Fifth Edition

THE Work Book
Getting the Job You Want

Instructor's Guide

J. Michael Farr

GLENCOE
McGraw-Hill

New York, New York   Columbus, Ohio   Mission Hills, California   Peoria, Illinois

Copyright © 1995, 1987 by Glencoe/McGraw-Hill. All rights reserved. Permission is granted to reproduce the material contained herein on the condition that such material be reproduced only for classroom use; be provided to students, teachers, and families without charge; and be used solely in conjunction with *The Work Book*. Any other reproduction, for use or sale, is prohibited without prior permission of the publisher.

Send all inquiries to:
Glencoe/McGraw-Hill
15319 Chatsworth Street
P.O. Box 9609
Mission Hills, California 91346-9609

ISBN 0-02-668451-9 (Student Text)
ISBN 0-02-668452-7 (Instructor's Guide)

Printed in the United States of America.

3 4 5 6 7 8 9 DBH 99 98 97

CONTENTS

FOREWORD	iv
INTRODUCTION	v
Why *The Work Book* Works	vi
Dealing with Special Populations	viii
The First Session	xii
TEACHING SUGGESTIONS	xvii
CHAPTER ONE	
Employer Expectations Measuring Up	1
CHAPTER TWO	
The DataTrakt® A Pocket Full of Power	5
CHAPTER THREE	
Applications Screening Yourself into the Running	9
CHAPTER FOUR	
JIST Cards A Taste of Your Talents	19
CHAPTER FIVE	
Telephone Contacts Dialing for Dollars	23
CHAPTER SIX	
The Interview For Rave Reviews	27
CHAPTER SEVEN	
Finding Job Leads Uncovering the Hidden Jobs	33
CHAPTER EIGHT	
Resumes Make Your REZ-oo-MAY Pay	39
CHAPTER NINE	
Organizing Your Job Search Ready, Set, Go!	43
ANNOTATED BIBLIOGRAPHY	45
Assessment Materials	45
Job-Search Books	45
Career Information Books	46
Instructor Materials	46

FOREWORD

This Instructor's Guide is intended for use with the fifth edition of *The Work Book: Getting the Job You Want*. The new text features updated content and an improved design. Revised chapters on job applications, interviews, and the DataTrakt now reflect the impact of antidiscrimination statutes like the Americans with Disabilities Act and immigration reform. Other chapters have been reorganized and trimmed so that now throughout the text illustration tracks sequentially with content. The new design features halftone photo illustration and models shaped by computer applications. Even more importantly, the design incorporates graphic devices that now make it possible for users to quickly locate and review the best of their job-search statements. The bold vertical bars throughout the text highlight each user's "book within a book," their personal collection of statements designed to show employers why they would be ideal employees.

For its part, this guide has mainly gotten a face lift. Little more was necessary. So many instructors have been so enthusiastic about its exercises that most of them have been left untouched. The reproducible forms, however, have been replaced to track with changes in the text.

If you haven't read *The Work Book* or don't have it nearby while perusing this guide, you will surely be lost. I suggest that you do go through *The Work Book* yourself before trying to teach it to others. Don't just read it; respond to it. Fill in the blanks. Do the exercises. Get on the telephone yourself and look for job leads. If you do these things, you'll be a far better instructor of others.

The Work Book was designed to help people find jobs. It is direct, concrete, practical, and even repetitive (purposely so). For now, it is enough to say that *The Work Book* is special because it is based on principles and techniques that actually increase the ability of job seekers to find jobs.

This guide will provide you with ideas, exercises, and approaches for using *The Work Book* in various contexts, such as classrooms, workshops, and individual counseling. Of course, you are in a far better position to adapt the material to your specific setting than I am. Feel free to personalize the ideas so that they fit your needs. Write in the margins. Insert your own ideas. Experiment, solve problems, adapt, be self-directed, enjoy, do.

J. Michael Farr

INTRODUCTION

Let me tell you about how I got my first job. I needed real money—about $10. So, I went out and asked for a job. The procedure was very simple. In the summer I asked people if I could mow their yards. In the winter I asked them if I could shovel their walks. If the grass was growing or there was snow on the walks, I was in demand. I could always earn "big money" on snowy days just by carrying my shovel around. My younger brother helped me. We'd walk up to doorways of houses with unshoveled walks and get work from every third door or so. No one ever asked us to fill out an application. Can you imagine that?

Apparently there was a high demand for reasonably polite kids who mowed and shoveled. This demand occurred because people heard from others that we shoveled walks and mowed lawns. The word got around. We never even had to read the want ads. When we wanted more money, we asked our customers who else needed to have work done.

Sometime between these first jobs and my graduation from college, I forgot how to find a job. Then, after a long period of time, I rediscovered a unique and effective job-finding process—the same one I'd used when I was ten years old.

Whether you are 10, 20, or 50 years old, to get a job you must

- want to work,
- decide where and when to look,
- present yourself well,
- tell people what you want to do, and
- ask people if you can help them (and if you can't, who can).

It sounds very easy, but there are complications. For one thing, some people do not want to work in the traditional employer-employee sense. And face it, some people don't want to work, period. In either of these cases, your best efforts in helping people find jobs should not be spent on these kinds of people.

Then there's the matter of the job seeker's knowing what he or she wants to do. This subject is not emphasized in *The Work Book* since there are so many good assessment tools now available from other sources. However, the successful job seeker doesn't knock on someone's door on a snowy day only to say, "I'm not sure what it is you might want me to do, but I'm here anyway." The successful job seeker says, "I want to shovel the snow on your walk," which is a far more effective approach to getting a job.

Knowing where, when, and how to look for a job is relatively easy when the job is shoveling snow. Apparently the process is more difficult for other jobs. At least people act as though they don't understand the process, and certainly many of the "normal" job-search techniques don't help matters any, misleading as they often are. In fact, many job-search guides advise job seekers to use only those techniques (personnel offices, for example) that are least effective.

Another complication is depression, which is often the reason why people don't look long enough or hard enough for the jobs they want. This depression isn't clinical depression (*i.e.*, the "I think I'm going to kill myself" variety) but a milder form ("I think I'll wash the car today—there aren't any jobs out there anyway, and everyone says the unemployment rate's so high"). Perhaps this sort of attitude results from a fear of talking to people, but I suspect there's more to it. "Experts" at the unemployment office, employment agencies, and in the newspapers always seem to be saying how tough things are. These messages are often not very encouraging—and the experts should know! Let's face it—looking for work is difficult. It's fraught with rejection and anxiety.

When you're a kid and just want money for a fish tank, it's easy to get motivated. "Real" jobs mean more somehow, and things become more complicated. That's why we wrote *The Work Book*. It's also why others need you to help them relearn how to do for themselves what they knew how to do when they were ten years old.

Why *The Work Book* Works

Several things make *The Work Book* a unique tool for job seekers. It is the only book of which the authors are aware that is completely based on job-search techniques that have been used in a highly effective job-search *program*. Since 1973 the authors have operated job-search programs in which 70–90 percent of the participants have found jobs. (Over half of these people have found jobs within 4–5 weeks of beginning the program.) Many of these participants have been "hard-core" unemployed. Many others have been people who live in areas with high unemployment rates. While this guide has not been designed to duplicate these job-search programs exactly, it does describe many of the same techniques used in them.

A research study has indicated that the materials in *The Work Book* did significantly increase the success rates of job seekers. (See *A Survey of Staff and Organizations Using JIST Materials and Job-Search Techniques* from the Research Department of the Community Service Council of Metropolitan Indianapolis, Inc.) This is meaningful because the effectiveness of so many of the job-search books on the market can't be documented. The study documents the assessments of instructors, who noted substantial increases in the job-seeking effectiveness of those who used *The Work Book*. Following is an excerpt:

> "All respondents (instructors) currently using the materials agreed that the concepts and approaches developed by JIST were helpful to their staff and program. When asked how they would rate JIST concepts and materials as a potential job seeker, almost all felt that JIST was anywhere from helpful to excellent."

In summary, then, *The Work Book* is a practical text. It is based on techniques that work exceedingly well and is one of the very few books documented as a tool that improves job-search outcomes.

How The Work Book *Was Written*

The content of *The Work Book* evolved from a job-search workshop that took place in 1973. This workshop was a major component of a more comprehensive job-search program, which I later named JIST—Job Information and Seeking Training. Since then JIST has developed quite a track record and recruited a very talented staff, which has continued to develop innovative methods for finding jobs.

Over the years thousands of job seekers have used these same techniques to find jobs. These people continue to teach us what does and does not work well. So, you now have the benefit of that collective experience.

You also benefit from the fact that this is the fifth edition of *The Work Book*. The improvements made in each revision have been based on extensive feedback from users of our materials. We've tried hundreds of great ideas. We've kept those that did work and discarded those that didn't. (One thing you can't do with job seekers is suggest the same ineffective techniques twice.)

Because *The Work Book* originated in interactive and dynamic workshop settings, the material has several rather unconventional features. Many sections require some degree of active response from the reader. Although the style is quite friendly, the reader is often asked to do something specific, now.

The order of *The Work Book's* content also evolved from experience with job seekers, and more specifically from the ways in which they reacted to the various exercise sequences. The presentation is rather unconventional, beginning with an exercise that explores employers' expectations of applicants. Actual job-seeking techniques are not covered until considerably later in the text.

Remember that one of our goals is to change people's basic assumptions about how to look for work. Simply to present job-search techniques is not enough. Knowing what employers expect can have a profound effect on those job seekers who internalize this knowledge and act upon it. The interplay of information with self-involvement and problem-solving with insight are inherent parts of what we've attempted to do.

There are several special characteristics in the writing style itself:

- *Concreteness.* Much of the material suggests a specific way of doing things or requires the job seeker to formulate a response or plan. The purpose is to move the job seeker toward action and away from reflection or contemplation.

- *Simplicity.* While the approaches presented by *The Work Book* are valid for college graduates, the writing style should be comprehensible to most people who read at or above the tenth-grade reading level. The techniques themselves have been modified for use by nonreaders.

- *Repetitiveness.* You will notice that several very basic points are repeated throughout *The Work Book*. This has been done because these points are so very important. For instance, an employer's expectations for a job seeker, once thoroughly understood, will affect how a job seeker approaches the entire process of job hunting. This one understanding, if thoroughly incorporated into the behavioral responses of job seekers, will probably lead to success. It is better to know a few things thoroughly and use them well than to know many things and use them ineffectively.

- *Respect.* None of our material "talks down" to the reader, which is why most adults and youths will find it relevant. We don't target a specific group of readers, nor do we avoid certain taboos. We've tried to deal with the very real fears that many job seekers have about their pasts, as well as the problems job seekers are likely to encounter in what is not always a fair and kind system.

- *Problem Solving.* There's not much we haven't heard excuse-wise. A problem is not a problem if a solution is found. We acknowledge a problem as such and give possible suggestions for solving it.
- *Self-direction.* Self-direction means "doing for yourself," which is what we encourage our readers to do. We'll help, but they've got to do.
- *Fun.* While *The Work Book* is hardly recreational reading (a job search being the serious task it is), we've tried to have some fun with parts of the content. The tone may help to relieve some of the tedium of the job-search process.

For Whom The Work Book *Was Written*

The audience for *The Work Book* can't be easily defined. *The Work Book* is for job seekers, all of whom seem to share common needs. While the text's reading level is moderate, it will not offend most adults. Teenagers should have no trouble with it. (Many instructors have been very successful using *The Work Book* with that group.) Some people do not have the discipline, inclination, or reading ability to use a book at all. These people will need individual help. As previously mentioned, the job-search techniques themselves have been used by many nonreaders who were taught solely through verbal presentations. At the other end of the spectrum, many job seekers have studied *The Work Book* on their own, without the benefit of a facilitator. In essence, *The Work Book* has been used with literally all categories of job seekers. It may well be more effective with some groups than with others, but I'm not at all sure.

Obstacles Facing Job Seekers

Perhaps most reasonably intelligent people could eventually figure out more effective methods of finding jobs. But, unfortunately, when left to their own devices, most job seekers do not do this. There are three reasons why:

1. *Experts.* We have all been trained to respect authorities, people who know more than we do because they sound as if they do or because of their credentials. Most job seekers do not question people such as the employment "specialist" at the local Employment Service Office who says there are "no openings." Who should know better, right? After having made the rounds of unemployment offices, personnel offices, and employment agencies, most job seekers feel very unemployable. They think that there are no jobs out there for them. The truth is often quite the opposite. Since jobs are often available, even in very hard times, it is important to know how to find them.

2. *Depression.* Maintaining a healthy sense of self while looking for a job is quite difficult. Looking for work becomes an isolating experience with lots of negative feedback ("Don't call us, etc."). Self-doubt becomes a serious problem that worsens with time. Even the best prepared and most qualified job seekers may then spend fewer hours looking and have fewer successful interviews. The more these people use techniques that get quick results, the less depression becomes an issue.

3. *Perception of need.* Since people rarely think about looking for a job when they are employed, the only time the need to do so becomes evident is after they have been unemployed for some time. Even then, because of the "experts" who say that most job seekers already know how to find jobs, many job seekers do not perceive potential benefits of new approaches to the job search.

The Work Book helps job seekers overcome these obstacles. How? First, it helps them to understand *how* to find jobs. Then, it instills in them the self-trust and decision-making skills that job seekers need to motivate them to *act*.

The Importance of the Instructor

For most people, finding a job is very hard work. Teaching other people to find jobs is harder, one step removed. It can also be very rewarding. The JIST approach can be taught fairly easily once you know the basics. Transferring this information to a person who needs it is not that complex. However, the instructor should be an active facilitator, which is where a good instructor comes in. Remember that it is what job seekers *do* with the information that is important, not what they *know*.

Job hunting is an interactional art in which the employer's decision to hire (or not to hire) the applicant is usually made in a fairly irrational manner during an interview. There are, however, two things we can do that will greatly affect the outcome of an interview:

1. Assist job seekers in organizing their job-search time so that they can find far more job leads and, hence, obtain more interviews.

2. Prepare job seekers to perform more effectively in interviews.

While job seekers can learn how to do both of these things by reading a book, the active involvement of an instructor can make a significant difference in how effectively they use what they learn. Let me give you an example. I can read up on how to handle a job interview and even practice in my mind how I would respond to different questions. But if I had someone play the employer in a mock interview with me, I'd have to *apply* what my mind had absorbed. That would be something quite different. If I took this a step further and staged this interview in front of people who would provide a friendly critique of my performance, then I'd create a level of anxiety similar to what I would feel in a real interview. I would learn that I could handle the anxiety and improve my performance. I would also learn to respond appropriately to unexpected situations. I would be far better prepared for a job interview than job seekers who hadn't practiced interviewing. Some of them might even be better qualified for a particular job, but whoever claimed that hiring was an entirely rational process?

A person who provides a job seeker with support, instructional guidance, and the inevitably necessary "push," also plays a role that can't be replicated by even the best of books. As an instructor you can give things more meaning, which sometimes makes the difference between a job seeker's getting a job or not.

How The Work Book *Differs from Other Job-Search Approaches*

Let me first sort out the major categories of vocational materials:

- *Assessment devices.* These include interest and abilities tests and other systems that tell us what we are good at and what we want to do.
- *Career exploration materials.* These describe the facets of various jobs. They inform us of the training required, working conditions, pay, employment projections, and the like.
- *Job-search materials.* These tell how to get a job, once defined.
- *Job-retention information.* Items that fall into this category tell us how to keep a job once we have found one. They also frequently suggest ways to get ahead on that job.

While this listing is simplistic, it may be helpful in defining just where *The Work Book* fits in—in the job-search category. Although *The Work Book* does not help the user define a job objective, some of the content might be of help in this area.

As you examine many of the available books on the subject, you will often find the four categories intertwined. Some are enjoyable to read and contain a lot of information. But what do you do with it? Too often the books that sell well off bookstore shelves are fun to read but do not provide practical advice or ways to use their ideas. While few would accuse *The Work Book* of being fun to read, it does provide the "nitty-gritty" techniques needed to find a job in a step-by-step way, fast.

There is another cluster of books (perhaps more accurately a subcategory) that deserves mention. It consists of books that emphasize one aspect of the job search, such as the job interview or the resume. This contrasts with *The Work Book*, which covers a variety of topics. Since these other books treat one topic in depth, many of them are excellent supplemental resources.

Dealing with Special Populations

This section of the Introduction was written so that I might share some of my experience in teaching the principles presented in *The Work Book* to members of special groups. Please bear in mind that, due to the unique nature of the job search, some of the "special" groups I've defined in this section are not at all disadvantaged in the traditional sense.

The concepts presented in *The Work Book* can be understood by most people. This is because much of the content evolved from oral presentations. While considerable adjustments were made as the material was written down, the book was based largely on a question-response format, and the style was kept conversational. For these reasons, *The Work Book* has been used successfully with thousands of job seekers, many of whom were part of quite heterogeneous groups.

The problem with any how-to book is that while it may be very good as written for some people, it may have to be modified for others. For example, a book that can be easily read by Joe may be difficult for Jenny. The fact is that no single product is right for everyone. This is as it should be. Any product has its compromises, including *The Work Book*.

The following sections give tips on providing special assistance. Please note that the categories of job seekers are presented in no particular order. And do forgive me for any comments that might appear to be less than sensitive. My interest here is purely in the reality of what works.

Unemployed Professionals

To make a point, I've chosen to begin with a group of people very few consider to have "special needs"—those with above-average skills. As a group, persons who have special training, education, and experience are harder to instruct than are those with less impressive credentials. For one thing, "specialists" are often more rigid and, thus, far less likely to follow instructions. For another, they are often accustomed to having others do more routine tasks for them. This is particularly true of job seekers displaced from higher-level corporate jobs.

Here are a few tips for dealing with this group.

- *If possible, ask these people to assist others.* Help might be given in such tasks as the preparation of resumes and JIST cards. Interestingly, the helpers have as much or more to gain than those they assist.
- *Insist they do the most basic of tasks.* Do not assume they can do anything well; have them demonstrate their proficiency. For example, some of the most sophisticated resistance to making telephone contacts has come from very educated people. They claim the technique can't possibly work, or they insist on using their own approach first. These objections are smoke screens. Chances are that these people are frightened.
- *Provide access to supplemental reading and/or deal with special issues on an individual basis.* For example, a job seeker applying for an advanced position may need to spend more time and effort in resume preparation than would someone looking for an entry-level job.

Nonreaders

If the person really cannot read at all (which is unlikely), a book of any kind will have limited use at best. However, if you have such a person in your class, it is very important that you do many verbal drills of *The Work Book* materials in class. Also, although it's not often done, parts of *The Work Book* might be read aloud.

JIST staff members have presented the content verbally many times. I'm sure that between this guide and *The Work Book* itself an effective curriculum could be put together.

Those with Limited Academic Skills

For our purposes here, the primary limitations are poor reading and poor verbal skills. *The Work Book* easily lends itself to use by persons with poor reading skills. For example, even poor readers can benefit greatly from the DataTrakt. While it will take them a great deal of time to complete the booklet, once it has been filled out, the information can be copied onto any application form. The DataTrakt makes it possible for such individuals to fill out applications without assistance.

Other sections of *The Work Book*, such as the first chapter, do not require extensive reading. So, such material can be approached in digestible, though laborious, segments. In respect to the other eight chapters, review them yourself beforehand with an eye toward passages that might cause trouble for poor readers. Then ask those people to read the material as a homework assignment.

Often, a poor reader's family or friends can help him or her with outside reading assignments. Since this assistance is given by others, most of the class time can be devoted to discussions and to reinforcement of the material assigned as homework.

What if all members of your group are poor readers? In this case, present the more difficult passages orally. However, don't spend all of your class time interpreting *The Work Book*. Be sure to allow yourself opportunities to correct problems that may arise and to answer questions.

Resisters

It is most difficult to teach job-search skills to those who, for one reason or another, don't wish to work. Do present a few of the standard rationales (such as, "You may need this later"), but don't expect miracles. Concentrate your attention instead on those in your class who do want to work, and use your creativity to minimize the disruptions of the others.

For example, when choosing persons to take on leadership or participatory roles, omit no one. Include even those who don't seem interested. Such people may soon learn that they will be unexpectedly asked to perform, and, as a result, they often begin to get involved rather than look foolish.

I often assign a homework task and announce that it will be reviewed in small groups during the next session. If you continually mix the groups randomly, someone who often fails to complete the assignment becomes an annoyance to peers, who then exert pressure to conform.

Even if a resister doesn't "tone down," remember that it is never appropriate to embarrass people publicly (intentionally, that is). It's far better to set up the environment in such a way that they embarrass themselves.

For those who can read but don't like to, keep the assignments short and make them as action-oriented as possible. Make an effort to relate what was read to what was learned through class work and/or outside experience.

Persons with Limited Work Experience

Much content in *The Work Book* will be of particular value to people who haven't had much work experience. Take, for example, the JIST card, which concisely presents a job seeker's skills and abilities. The card (unlike a resume) lets people emphasize their strengths as opposed to their lack of experience.

In terms of teaching techniques themselves, refer to an employer's expectations as presented in Chapter 1 of *The Work Book*. Reiterate the fact that previous work experience is not at the top of most employers' expectations lists. It's not even second. But the issue will come up (probably in an interview). The person with limited work experience should be prepared to address this apparent problem in a positive manner. Ways in which he or she might respond include the following:

- "I'll start at the bottom and work up!"
- "I learn fast. Since this is my first job, I want to make sure I do well."
- "I'm not afraid of hard work."

- "I haven't learned any bad habits yet, so I'll learn to do things your way!"

The fact is that job seekers of limited experience will often be hired—if they present themselves well. This is a very important point to emphasize when dealing with relatively inexperienced workers.

A lack of previous work experience also will affect a person's job objective. He or she will often need to break an ideal job into a series of short-term objectives. For example, a person just out of high school or college may want to own a restaurant. He or she should first define restaurant ownership as a long-term objective, since it is unlikely that someone in this situation would be able to go into business without having had some basic experience first. It is probable, however, that a job obtained at an entry level (dishwasher, for example) could be parlayed into an assistant manager's position, and so forth. Once the short-range objectives have been attained, the long-term objective is within reach. Helping students define these steps towards a long-term objective can be most rewarding for the instructor. Do it when you can.

Students

Because of a disenchantment with school or an enthusiasm for the idea of working, some students may be thinking about dropping out. The only responsible position for you to take in teaching job-seeking skills to young people is this: carefully avoid encouraging anyone to drop out of school to find a job. Stress the value of finishing school, particularly for those in high school. And encourage the acquisition of after-school jobs that are not likely to lead to full-time employment or that emphasize self-employment, such as painting houses or mowing lawns.

Like everyone else, students should formulate long-term career objectives. This will provide them with the incentive to finish school and, perhaps, to obtain more training. Do bear in mind that many young people do not have a sense of objectives. Most experiment with different jobs before settling into a career or area of work, which often doesn't occur until their midtwenties. This process of job exploration is not likely to change significantly even for those who, as teens, define tentative career objectives. But such guidance can facilitate the transition to a stable career path.

Dropouts and Unemployed Youth

The unemployment rate among 16–22 year olds who are not in school is exceeded only by the unemployment rate of minorities within that same age range. All such young persons, unskilled and often uneducated, have limited access to even entry-level jobs. There are many problem areas for these people besides lack of skills. They often have very poor self-presentation skills, have not actively looked for work in some time, and haven't the faintest idea of what they want to do for an employer. Some may also not *want* to work in the way work is traditionally defined.

With respect to those who don't want to work, there is no point in teaching them job-seeking skills. However, do realize that, having had undesirable jobs in the past, many people are at a loss when it comes to naming positive aspects of work. In such cases, career assessment can often be a motivating force.

For young people who *do* want to work, there is hope in the fact that most of their peers are not using the effective, direct-contact techniques outlined in *The Work Book*. Let me give you an example. My office is in an urban area. Within walking distance are thousands of unemployed persons. At this very moment in time, there are several tasks that I would pay a young person to do. In this work there might or might not be the potential for a full-time job. I'd say the situation is a fairly typical one for most small businesses. In the past year only two people have dropped in looking for entry-level jobs. Unfortunately, both lacked self-presentation skills.

As do people of older age groups, young persons need to plan an active job search. They, like others, should actively use the sources of job leads discussed in Chapter 7 of *The Work Book*. If they are presently unemployed, young men and women are in a good position to contact small businesses about odd jobs, which sometimes may become permanent if done well. For example, offering to clean an employer's parking lot will bring the young person to the attention of that employer. These odd jobs often provide an opportunity for young people to present themselves well and display their value to a potential employer.

For young persons who have an interest in specific trades or occupations, it may be worthwhile to seek a position where a more experienced worker will teach them the trade. This concept, which was used for centuries in craft work, is still used in some settings. There are many experienced workers who work independently but might consider taking on an enthusiastic intern with the right approach.

Adults

In *The Work Book*, we've tried to treat the job search as an issue for job seekers in general rather than for a specific subgroup of job seekers. For this reason, no adaptation is required for using the book with adults.

For use with adults who have an immediate need to find a job, we recommend that the job seeker first get an easy-to-obtain job that will stave off economic disaster. In saying this, please understand that I am not undervaluing the interim job nor suggesting that it be obtained in a manipulative way. Acquiring an interim job needs to be approached responsibly. To seek such a job cynically or flippantly would be contrary to the approach endorsed in Chapter 1 of *The Work Book*.

Employers look for dedication and ability even in low-paid, entry-level jobs. For employees who do well in them, such positions can be stepping-stones to jobs offering more responsibility and remuneration. Consider the case histories of two adults with whom I have worked:

Railroad laborer:

Male, 36 years old, out of work for four months. He was two months behind on his house payments, had two children, and no source of income. His solution was to get short-term jobs from a temp service, and later, a job as a night security guard. His income was lower than it had been on the railroad, but he could meet his personal obligations while looking for a better job during the day. He eventually was promoted to a supervisory position at the security company and also found jobs as an independent painting contractor. Today his income is slightly above what it was on the railroad, and he appears to be satisfied with his current situation.

Nurse's aide:

Female, 23 years old, unemployed for over a year. She wanted to work in a hospital where she could use her training as a nurse's aide but, after several unsuccessful attempts, had given up on finding a position in the medical field. Because she came from a large family and had considerable informal experience working with children, she looked for and obtained a job as a teacher's aide at a child care center. Her medical training was an asset there and, though the pay was low, she preferred this job to her earlier ones. She is now seeking a position in a children's ward of a hospital. Since she has had one year of successful work experience at the child care center, her present employer will give her an excellent reference.

Older Job Seekers

Persons in their middle years may present unique job-search problems. Those who have been displaced from their established careers often want to begin anew in a different field. Often their initial attempts at defining a new career are irrational. Thus, before deciding just what they want to do, persons in this situation should assess their skills carefully and then weigh the various benefits and disadvantages of their options. Because an emotionally based decision made too hastily may have lasting negative consequences, moving slowly is often a good approach. Of course, a stopgap job may be needed in the meantime.

Many areas have organizations that provide specialized services for people in these situations. Refer your older job seekers to the ones with good reputations and reasonable fees.

Job seekers over 40 often feel that they are discriminated against by employers, and there is some evidence that they are. On average, it takes older job seekers 60 percent longer to find work than job seekers in their twenties or thirties.

As suggested in *The Work Book,* this problem should be addressed by job seekers in such a way that their age can be presented as a benefit. Here are some examples:

- "I am a very responsible person with years of experience. Because I've lived here for over ten years, I intend to stay in the area and seek a position that offers growth potential."
- "Now that my children are grown, I prefer a challenging job in an interesting environment. I'm willing and able to start in a position from which I can advance, based on my performance."
- "While most people over 35 change jobs every four years or so, I am seeking a position that I can make into a career for the next ten (or more) years. I have no interest in job-hopping and will work hard to move up within an organization rather than leave it."

Older workers, then, will need to define the problems they may face with employers and provide solutions—as must all job seekers.

Minorities

Whether it is race, religious affiliation, or something else, some employers do discriminate against certain groups, either by not hiring them at all or by restricting their access to certain positions. This is an immoral and unsupportable stance. On a one-to-one basis, however, I suspect that discriminatory hiring practices are less prevalent than many people assume. Most job seekers will use any handy rationale to justify their inability to find jobs. The attitude that minority status (or gender, lack of experience, etc.) is the problem can be a devastatingly effective rationale for giving up.

If a job seeker belongs to a minority group, my suggestion is for that person to act as if this is an irrelevant factor—which it is. The odds are very high that adhering to the essential concepts of *The Work Book* will greatly help any job seeker meet an employer's expectations and get hired. As an instructor, your task is to eliminate students' excuses for not trying and to foster success.

Persons with Mental or Physical Disabilities

Mentally retarded persons have proven themselves to be good workers in a variety of settings. Their limited success in finding jobs is often the result of their inability to look for work actively, to present themselves well, or both.

However, the major problem I have found with respect to this group is not with the job seekers themselves but with family members or nonprofit agencies that have a vested interest in limiting the independence of their charges. Within families the motive is often to avoid a situation where the retarded person might fail, but the consequence is frequently a restriction of the person's right to take chances and learn from both failure and success. As for the agencies, I have worked in a rehabilitation facility that kept persons capable of getting and keeping jobs in private industry locked into positions that generated revenues for the facility. I am not suggesting that all such facilities operate this way. Admittedly, there is some good work being done in sheltered workshops. But many of those who work in them could be absorbed into the mainstream—if special assistance in acquiring outside jobs were available.

Often, working with persons who are mentally retarded requires more active personal assistance from an instructor. These people may need help developing a JIST card, learning to arrange transportation to interviews, and even finding job leads. For example, at various times I have gone with a person by bus to an interview site and waited outside.

In some cases, you may need to contact prospective employers personally. When they know how to handle them, employers often respond positively to persons who are mentally retarded. For example, I've told an employer to be sure to tell the new employee exactly what was to be done and to correct the worker's mistakes verbally and matter-of-factly. Once "permission" to do this was given, all was well.

Persons who are mentally ill present unique problems. Review with the job seeker the types of previous work situations in which he or she achieved only limited success. Then encourage him or her to avoid jobs where these conditions are present. In many cases the person may also know which job-related factors contribute to his or her stability. Positions in which these characteristics are present should be sought.

In all cases a person should be trained to perceive a job as a situation that is an economic exchange based on performance. He or she should avoid conflicts with others and not ask for special consideration.

Those with physical disabilities should make sure that their career objectives are realistic from a physical point of view. The job seeker should bear in mind that if a condition will not affect on-the-job performance, it is not a disability. If a disability is visible or will have an effect on his or her work, the job seeker should present the facts honestly but in a way that minimizes any negative aspects.

Other Special Groups

Guidelines for working with many other special groups could be presented, but space limitations require brevity. Your best guides to what is best are your common sense, a willingness to try things, and an openness to learning from job seekers themselves what works.

The First Session

This section of the Introduction provides you with some tips on how to approach your first session with a new group of job seekers. There is a lot to do and know, and you want to be at least one step ahead of your students.

Preparation

Before you even say, "Good morning," there are a number of things you need to do to facilitate any group. You should

- have an agenda you can handle,
- know what your objectives are,
- have the facility set up,
- have all handouts and other materials ready, and
- be prepared for the unexpected.

Let's explore each of these briefly.

Have an Agenda You Can Handle It is very important to have worked out a reasonably detailed agenda of what you will do and when. This may seem basic, but many instructors skip this important step.

Agendas are guides to help you use your time effectively and efficiently. They are not straitjackets. They can be altered as necessary.

If you are reasonably new to the content of job search, I suggest your agenda have several optional tasks, which can be inserted as time permits. (These can save you if you have some time to fill.) In planning your agenda, estimate how much time each component will take. Stick to the agenda as closely as you can. If you have time left, use your optional exercises.

Know What Your Objectives Are If you are working with people who don't yet know what they want to do, you have very different issues to deal with from an instructor of people who do know what they want to do. Those with the most at stake in learning how to find jobs are those who have an immediate need and desire to work. If your group consists of people who aren't planning to look for work in the near future (or aren't sure they want to work), your objectives will differ also. For these reasons, asking individual members of your group what they want or need to do is often a very good place to start in determining your instructional objectives.

Have the Facility Set Up Controlling the instructional environment can make the difference between sessions with alert, active, and involved participants and those that just don't seem to "take off." Consider the following measures:

- *Make sure your location is as interruption-free as possible.* Arrange for the class not to be interrupted with messages unless an emergency arises.

- *Control the temperature.* Avoid extremes of heat or cold. Remember, people perform best in rooms that are just a bit cool.
- *Arrange for movable, not fixed, seating so that various configurations (such as small groups) are possible.* Tables, I find, just get in the way (job seekers use them to separate themselves from others). I prefer to do without them. You can avoid the feel of a typical classroom (straight rows of chairs) by arranging the seating in a semicircle or similar setup.
- *Pick the best place for you.* This would be where you feel most comfortable. Walk around the room until you find the spot that suits you. Have everyone else move their chairs, if necessary. You are the instructor!
- *Serve refreshments, if you can.* In workshop settings, this is a nice touch that fosters social interaction.

Have All Handouts and Other Materials Ready

Handouts and training aids often make life easier for an instructor. Set aside a table of your own for these materials and maintain control of them. Here are more specifics.

- *Handouts.* Use as few as possible since they are often distracting and are rarely referred to after a session is over. If you do use some, pick those that require some activity on the part of the job seeker. Blank paper is one of my favorite handouts.
- *Pencils.* You'll need some, but consider whether you should supply them routinely to group members. Employers, as a rule, don't provide them to job seekers filling out applications. After the first session, neither should you.
- *Blackboards vs. flip charts.* The flip chart (consisting of large, blank sheets of paper) is far more flexible than a blackboard. The sheets can be torn off and saved or taped to walls. Also, keep in mind that flip charts may be prepared in advance. If you have access to them, don't overlook these handy tools.
- *Transparencies/slides.* Use whatever works for you. Just have the items well organized in advance so you can find what you want when you want it.

Be Prepared for the Unexpected
It always happens. Anticipate it. Don't get upset. Adapt. Use your creative, problem-solving abilities. Carry on.

Career Assessment

In the beginning of *The Work Book*, we speak of the need for the job seeker to have defined a job objective *before* starting to look for a job. This is important. *The Work Book* presents a very effective approach for developing job leads that will lead to job offers. But by design it avoids helping the reader develop a job objective as well.

So, what do you do about those in your group who haven't the faintest idea of what they want to do? Try one of the following options.

Ask for a Job Preference Statement Simply asking an undecided group member to state a preference falls under the category of not overlooking the obvious. The method is amazingly reliable compared to many others that are less direct. I am not suggesting that every person asked will have a well-informed response, but it is certainly a place to start.

Conduct an Informal Assessment Develop a simple form to help people compile a list of their likes and dislikes. These could be related to such areas as jobs held, school subjects, hobbies, and volunteer work. Upon examination, such lists often reveal a pattern. That pattern plus the response to the question *What sort of a job are you interested in?* can form the basis for some very functional career counseling.

Arrange for Formal Testing One source of free tests in many regions is the U.S. Employment Service, sometimes known as the Employment Security Division. This agency provides both interest and abilities tests. A variety of interest tests are used.

The General Aptitude Test Battery (GATB) is most often used as the test of basic abilities. Some free counseling is also provided, but the quality varies considerably. This is a good free resource, however, and should be used if available. The GATB is available only through your local Employment Service office and a few authorized locations. It is an old test and surely one of the most validated vocational tests ever developed. It tests various abilities such as math and fine motor coordination and matches scores to those of workers required to do well in various jobs. It is not an interest test and is not self-scored.

There are many other interest and abilities tests available and everyone has his or her preferences. Because I have a basic mistrust of the ultimate value of a test as compared to the judgments of those most affected by them, my preference is for tests that heavily involve the test taker in the conclusion made. There are several newer, self-scoring tests that do just this, and I'm sure better ones will evolve.

The Self-Directed Search (SDS) from Psychological Assessment Resources in Odess, Florida, is a good one in this category. This test and the occupational theories behind it have revolutionized the way most career interest tests are now constructed. It is probably the most widely used test of its type. It is an easy test to take and the new revision covers over 1,100 occupations. A low reading level version is available, as are Spanish and Vietnamese versions. The tests cost about a dollar each.

The Career Decision-Making System by the American Guidance Service, Circle Pines, Minnesota, is another test that is self-scoring and very actively involves the test taker. I like this test for use in groups with young people. The directions are somewhat more complex than those for the SDS, but it is still quite easy to use.

If a test is used, please put it into its proper perspective. No test should ultimately replace the judgment of the job seeker. People do have the right to fail in what you or I believe is an inappropriate job objective. We've been wrong before, as have the tests. I do think it is important to assist a job seeker in establishing a job objective that is reasonably achievable, whatever this means to you.

Career exploration is often a necessary part of defining a job objective. Most job seekers do not know enough about various jobs to make informed decisions about whether or not they would like them. The better tests provide references to career information systems. Most of these, in turn, are based on the *The Dictionary of Occupational Titles* and the Department of Labor's companion publications. All provide excellent supplemental information on careers. Additional career assessment and exploration materials are listed in the Annotated Bibliography beginning on page 00 of this guide.

Suggest Information Interviewing Another very useful assessment technique is information interviewing as described in Chapter 7 of *The Work Book* and in the teaching suggestions that appear in this guide for Chapter 6. A job seeker can use the interview for strictly exploratory purposes.

In summary, whatever the technique used, establishing a job objective prior to learning job-seeking skills is essential. Job seekers should keep their objectives flexible, though. Based on new information about a job or about themselves, job seekers may change their objectives. (Some people change their job objectives after having worked for a while, thus the phenomenon of the career change.)

Introductions

Even if you already know all the job seekers and they know each other, introducing yourself to them in a different way can help set the right tone. Here are the procedures that I use to get started.

- Keep the introduction informal but structured.
- Begin with an explanation of your objectives and the procedures for achieving them.
- Cover any logistics (rest breaks, for example).
- Go over the agenda very briefly.
- Elicit brief and superficial introductions from each person.

All this might take 15–60 minutes, depending on your situation. Let's now concentrate on the introduction process itself.

Conventional Introductions When involved in group settings, people expect to introduce themselves. Dread of standing up in a group is a common fear, so introductions should be made quickly and conventionally. Because you introduced yourself briefly at the beginning of the session, you should handle the group introductions. You could say, "I'd like each of you to tell us your name and where you're from." This would be followed by five-second self-introductions. While this is the conventional approach, it is also relatively meaningless. It has the advantage of being quick, but it has the disadvantage of being a totally forgettable experience for a newly formed group and an irrelevant one for a group in which the members know each other already. Regardless, go ahead and make your minimal introductions—it makes a useful contrast for what happens next.

Extended Introductions This form of introduction has been used many times with job seekers who previously knew each other, as well as with newly formed groups. You can even adapt it for use in very large groups.

Begin by introducing yourself. Present yourself as an "ex-job seeker" (unless, of course, you are presently looking for a job). State the following:

- Your name
- Something about your personal and family history
- Something about your educational experiences (good and bad)
- Something about your work history
- Something about your current situation
- Your job objective
- What you want to get out of the sessions

Here's an abbreviated example: "My name is John Smith. I grew up in a suburb of Chicago. There were five kids in my family, and I was the next to the youngest. That meant I learned early how to get attention—or be last in line for the pork chops! Still, I remember enjoying myself, and I guess I had a good childhood.

"I went to three high schools. I was something of a problem child at that age but grew out of it and went on to college and . . ."

If you do this right, it should take about 4–5 minutes. Since people never introduce themselves this way, your group's members will now know you as more of a peer than an authority figure. In addition, once you've finished, you will have modeled for them what you want them to do next. Before you proceed, though, open up the discussion so that anyone can ask you questions about your background.

Then tell them it's their turn to do the same thing in groups of four or five. On a flip chart, list all the items you want them to cover in their introductions. Alter the list as you wish, but don't include too many items. Tell the group members to allow from 4–6 minutes per person—no more, no less. (If necessary, they are to ask the shy people questions to fill up the time.)

As the groups proceed, move about and listen in. Avoid taking over a small group or getting too involved in a leadership role.

These introductions will take 30–45 minutes and are well worth the time. People get to talk about themselves, which is precisely what they will do in interviews later. They also get to know and trust one another in new ways, which will help greatly in subsequent exercises. If you handle the introductions well, you will have made a move toward building a functional group rather than a collection of unrelated individuals.

Once the introductions are taken care of, the group should be ready to tackle some preliminary exercises. These will set the stage for Chapter 1 of *The Work Book* by sorting out those who are truly serious about finding employment and acquainting them with some of the realities of today's job market. Try to do all four exercises.

• •

GETTING STARTED EXERCISE
Job Objectives and Related Skills

Objective/Rationale

This exercise is designed to provide each job seeker with knowledge of his or her self-presentation ability. If the group members are new to you, the exercise is also a time-efficient way for you to evaluate the validity of their job objectives and identify group members who will need individual attention.

Procedure

Step 1: Have one job seeker tell you his or her job objective.

Step 2: On the top of a large flip chart sheet, list his or her name and the job objective. Clarify as needed.

Step 3: Ask, "Why should an employer hire you?" You will probably get an unconvincing reply. List the responses and continue to ask "Why else?" until the job seeker runs out of responses. If the job seeker has done well, say so. If the answers were not convincing, ask the group, "Would you hire this person for this job?" If the answer is no, ask why not or what else they would need to know. Continue until you have enough reasons listed to justify hiring the person.

Step 4: Keep going until you have one flip chart sheet completed for each job seeker. You may wish to tape each completed sheet to the wall for future reference.

Step 5: Wrap it up. Comment on how quickly the group members "got the hang of things." Ask them what they learned. Ask for comments.

Note: For the types of information to be supplied here, refer to *The Work Book* chapter on JIST cards. But don't give the group the JIST-card format. Simply aim for at least five entries per person.

GETTING STARTED EXERCISE
Who Doesn't Want to Work?

Objective/Rationale

I don't want unwilling job seekers in my workshop sessions, so I often clarify everyone's involvement by offering the option of leaving. (Of course, if you are a classroom teacher, you probably won't be able to exercise this option.) Often I find that people who are ambivalent about working—because of fear of failing or some other reason—often make a quick and self-assertive decision to stay.

Procedure

Step 1: Say something like, "Oh yes, is there anyone here who doesn't want to be here?" This is always good for a laugh if you keep it light. You can also say, "Are there people here who are not sure they want to work?" If a few hands do go up, say, "Thanks for being honest. There are many reasons why people are not sure. Since this is a (class, workshop, or whatever) on getting a job, you may want to consider dropping out. You're welcome to stay, of course, but you will have to participate as a job seeker, as will everyone else."

Step 2: If they want to go, fine. Meet them during break, send them on their way, or take some other appropriate action. Do this right away. The others will then know you are serious in meeting your stated objectives—and theirs.

Introduction **XV**

GETTING STARTED EXERCISE

An Overview of the Job Search

Objective/Rationale

This exercise is designed, frankly, to impress job seekers with what they don't yet know. If you present a compelling and well-documented rationale for the benefits to be derived from participating in your sessions, you've attracted their attention.

Procedure

Step 1: "Bone up" on high-interest facts regarding the job search. Record your findings on 3" x 5" cards. (Thoroughly review Chapter 7 of *The Work Book*, and use its references liberally.)

Step 2: Do a brief presentation on areas of high interest, using graphics and flip charts. Here are some topics to cover.
- The average number of times people change jobs
- The average number of career changes expected
- Traditional job-seeking methods and their effectiveness rates. (A pie chart makes a lovely illustration of how ineffective they really are.)
- How people actually do find jobs
- The "hidden" job market, where so many unadvertised jobs are
- Why the job seeker who uses nontraditional techniques is often hired, while more experienced and even better qualified people are not

Step 3: Wrap up. Keep your comments brief, and encourage questions and discussion. The intent is to elicit interest in what is to come, not to provide final answers.

GETTING STARTED EXERCISE

Difficult Questions

Objective/Rationale

This exercise is intended to help group members realize how poorly prepared most of them are for a job interview. It should be conducted in a playful manner to maintain a high level of interest and avoid embarrassing any individuals.

Procedure

Step 1: Look through *The Work Book* chapter on interviews to get a list of interview questions to ask. Here is a short list of good ones:
- Why should I hire you?
- Tell me about yourself.
- What are your three most powerful skills that relate to this position?
- What would your former employers (or teachers or whoever) say about you?
- How much money do you expect to be paid?
- We are looking for someone with more experience (younger, older, etc.) than you. What do you have to offer over someone like that?
- Why do you want this job?
- What are your major weaknesses?

Step 2: Once the group is in session, quickly and without warning, ask a specific person to answer an interview question. Ask, "Why should I hire you, John?" John will, in all probability, respond with an "Uhhh" (or something just as impressive). If this is done correctly, it gets lots of laughs, since you should quickly put everyone on the spot.

Step 3: Just as quickly ask, "Are any of you willing to hire John based on his response?" Have the group evaluate his performance. If someone does do a good job, say so or encourage others in the group to do so.

• •

In Conclusion

I do hope the foregoing exercises and other information I've shared in this Introduction will help you use *The Work Book* more effectively. There is much more that could have been said, but I trust you will find that your own experiences and those of your group members will supplement what you have learned here.

Do realize that if you have read *The Work Book*, sought jobs yourself, and accumulated some life experience, you have much to offer others as an instructor. And your group members have much to offer, too. You don't have to provide all the answers. Turn questions back to your students. Ask them what they think. Harness the powers of their intellects, and you will all learn together.

TEACHING SUGGESTIONS

CHAPTER ONE

Employer Expectations
Measuring Up

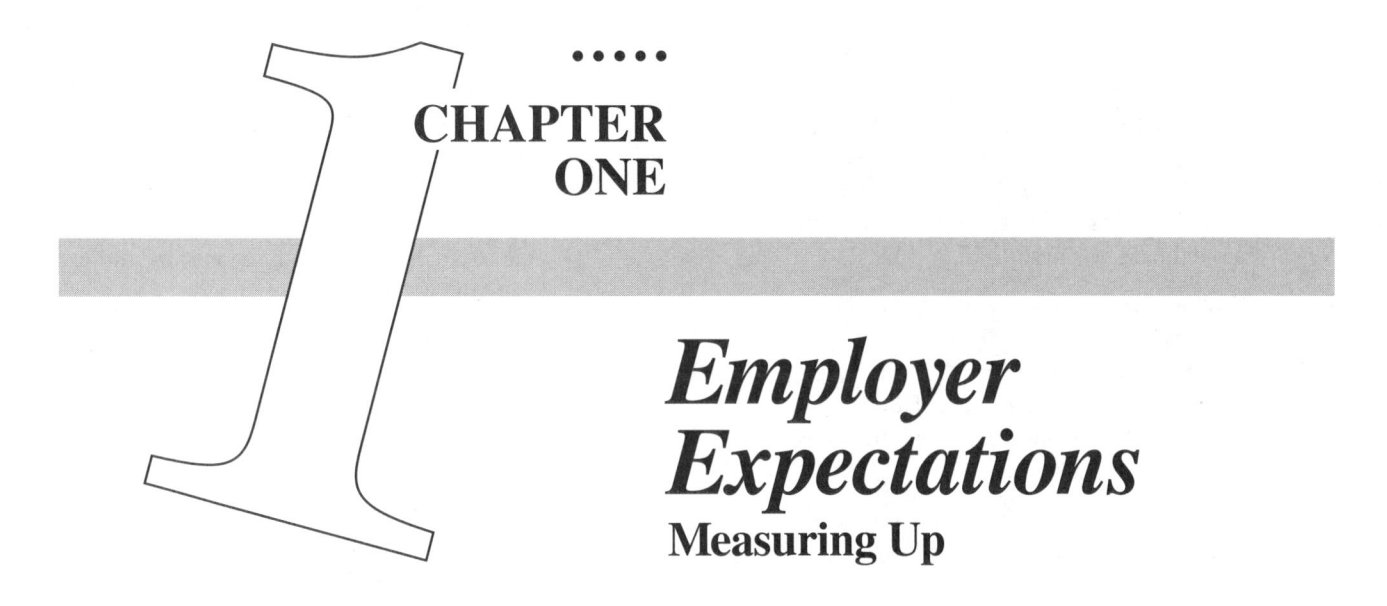

Chapter 1, "Employer Expectations," is a key chapter of *The Work Book*. It is a basis for much of what appears in subsequent chapters. The chapter presents the job seeker with a perspective often ignored in the more traditional literature. That is, the advice is not the usual advice, such as "Give a firm handshake and make good eye contact" or "Make sure you tell them you got an A in typing." Instead, Chapter 1 has been carefully constructed to place the job seeker in the employer's shoes. The question is posed, "What would you look for in a job seeker if you were the employer?"

Presenting the facts of what an employer wants would be much easier than posing this question—a paragraph would suffice. The job seekers would promptly forget the list and would surely not significantly change their attitudes or behaviors. But with the approach used in *The Work Book*, the facts come from the job seekers themselves, which allows the information to become internalized and then acted upon.

I have often noted a sincere and very real shift from the "I want a job" or "How much do you pay" position to the very natural "If you hire me, I will be a reliable worker for you" sort of response. This internal shift of reference points from "Give me" to "I offer" more truly reflects the actuality of an employer-employee relationship. Employers, job seekers learn, are much like everyone else. Because perceptions of the differences between "us" and "them" become less pronounced, job seekers also find employers less frightening and more human during interviews. As a result, interviews become comfortable exchanges rather than feared confrontations.

CORE EXERCISE
Employer Expectations

Objective/Rationale
Core exercises are those recommended above all others. In this particular core exercise, the job seekers are presented with the issue prior to being given the "answers." The exercise invites each job seeker to take on the role of the employer. In this capacity, the job seekers define what they think would be important to look for in a potential employee. This exercise is a clear example of how instructors *facilitate* by providing the basic structure. The instructor then leaves the conclusions unstated until the exercise has been completed.

Procedure

Step 1: Arrange to do this exercise *before* the job seekers read or have access to *The Work Book*. Prior knowledge will reduce the impact of the exercise.

Step 2: Introduce the exercise very simply. For example, say, "It is important to understand what an employer will look for in a job seeker. I want you to take on the role of an employer, and, as such, examine just what an employer really wants from you. In groups of four or five, I want you to give your group a name of a company and act like a personnel committee. You have to come up with a list of things you think are important to

Chapter 1   Employer Expectations   **1**

look for in a potential employee. Make the list as long as you can. Pick a recorder to list your ideas. It doesn't matter for now whether the ideas are good ones or not. You are just to list them for now, and we'll discuss them later. You have five minutes." (Of course, you may allow more time if you wish.)

Step 3: Without further explanation, you might leave the room. This is a simple brainstorming exercise, and your presence can hamper things because you're an "authority." Don't hang around to answer questions; the job seekers will figure things out eventually.

Step 4: Two minutes before the allotted time is up, come in and announce, "Two more minutes and we wrap it up."

Step 5: Precisely two minutes later say, "Okay, let's wrap up this part of the exercise," and do precisely that.

Step 6: Now instruct the job seekers to go on by saying, "Okay, now each group is to pick out the five or six most important criteria to be used in actually selecting an employee from a group of job seekers. You have five minutes to do this."

Step 7: Repeat your disappearing act, as in step 3 above.

Step 8: Repeat steps 4 and 5 above.

Step 9: Say something like, "Now I want you to pick out the top three criteria and list them in order from the most important to the least. Remember, select the ones you feel are most important in screening a good employee. You have another five minutes."

Step 10: Repeat steps 4 and 5.

Step 11: This is the hard part. Each group now has a list of its three most important criteria in order of importance. Your job is to come up with a group consensus as to the top three choices. Here are some suggested approaches.

- Ask for a volunteer to lead the class in a discussion to figure out the rankings. This allows you to relax while they have a lively discussion.
- A representative from each group can read that group's list. You then write the items on a flip chart. There will surely be some similar, although differently worded, entries that can be combined. When the list is complete, ask for a show of hands for "first place" for each entry. Then count responses. This could decide the winner. A more mathematically correct (and also more complicated) method is to assign three points for each first-place vote, two points for each second-place vote, and one for each third-place vote. Allow each person only one vote for each place—first, second, and third. Count the votes and add up the totals.
- Or, perhaps you have a better way.

Step 12: Wrap up the exercise by comparing the job seekers' list of criteria with the list of employer expectations in *The Work Book*. Your group may have come up with some or all of the survey responses. If so, congratulate the job seekers for their great intellect. If not, console yourself with the hope that they are now prepared to get much more out of what you will ask them to do next, which is . . .

Step 13: Homework. That's right, tell the job seekers to complete Chapter 1, "Employer Expectations."

Note: Feel free to adapt this exercise as you wish, but first try it as it is described here, if you can. It's a powerful exercise, if done well.

EMPLOYER EXPECTATIONS EXERCISE

Survey of Employers (#1)

Objective/Rationale

In this exercise job seekers are to go out and survey employers to determine what they look for when screening applicants. The employers' responses may or may not match those in *The Work Book*. Regardless, this activity will surely provide a good learning experience. A hidden objective is to desensitize job seekers to contacts with employers by setting up low-risk contacts.

Procedure

Step 1: I suggest that Chapter 1 of *The Work Book* be completed prior to the survey.

Step 2: Avoid "overorganization." Instead, ask the group to explain the questions on the survey, the survey process itself, and the analysis of results. Suggest the use of a simple survey form that has no more that 5–10 simple questions.

Step 3: Emphasize that the survey's objective is to determine the surveyed employers' three top expectations and to compare them with those listed in *The Work Book*. Tell the group that they have an hour or less to design the survey form and the basic process. Use small subgroups if you wish. Each can do an assigned task.

Step 4: Remind job seekers that an employer is anyone to whom another person reports. Remember that small businesses and even relatives are likely to be most accessible. Such contacts are to be encouraged.

Step 5: Each job seeker should visit at least one or two employers. Remind the job seekers to be on their best behavior, dress appropriately, and say, "Thank you" (all of which are related to employer expectations, by the way). Also, remind them to keep an eye open for any job opening in which they might be interested. Finding an opening this way happens more often than you might imagine.

Step 6: When your people all come back, a good discussion should be easy to initiate. Just ask, "Well, what are employers' expectations?"

Step 7: Pull together (or, rather, have the job seekers pull together) the data and determine the top three employer expectations as indicated by the survey responses.

EMPLOYER EXPECTATIONS EXERCISE
Survey of Employers (#2)

Dick Gaither, JIST's former Director of Training, submitted this exercise. It is similar to the previous survey exercise. Dick has also submitted some of the exercises that appear later in this guide.

Goals

- To desensitize students to face-to-face contact with employers
- To reinforce the content/concepts presented in *The Work Book*
- To generate external activity. This will make the students more responsible for their own performances and, therefore, less dependent on the instructor.
- To show participants that the job market has very few norms and that the employer's demands are often vague
- To inform participants about employer expectations before the participants go on their own interviews

Materials

- Pencils and paper (enough for each job seeker to have five sheets)
- Telephone books—one for every three students

Procedure

Step 1: Have the participants choose five work sites to visit. (The type of work being done at the site need not relate to the type of work that the participant is seeking.)

Step 2: Have the students write down the name, address, and phone number of each business at the top of a sheet of paper.

Step 3: Under each business, have the students list the following questions:
- What do you expect of a good worker?
- What are five specific skills needed in this work?
- What are five specific personality traits needed by workers in this field?

Step 4: Tell the students that they are to do the following:
- Try to learn the name of the person in charge.
- Talk with the person in charge and ask the questions listed above.
- List the responses on the work sheet.
- List the name of the person contacted and his or her title or area of responsibility.
- Report the findings to the class on the next day of instruction.

Step 5: Review the class activity. Compare and contrast the different methods utilized. Identify problem areas. Try to show the general uniformity of basic expectations. Appropriate connections to *The Work Book* should be made.

EMPLOYER EXPECTATIONS EXERCISE
Discussion

Objective/Rationale

Group discussions can be valuable if the participants keep to the subject. These discussions can provide a medium for asking questions, stating differing opinions, examining varying perspectives, and gaining a more thorough understanding of the issue discussed. Here are a few suggestions for supplementing *The Work Book* in a group setting.

Procedure

Step 1: Before you have the job seekers read Chapter 1, ask them to do the following:

- State why this topic (employer expectations) is an issue for job seekers.
- Give examples of their previous contacts with employers and tell whether or not they felt they met the employers' expectations.
- Break the group into smaller groups to discuss these points.

Step 2: Do the following activities after the students have read Chapter 1.

- Have the large group break into smaller groups. Each group is to develop a case study of a job seeker who meets one or two expectations but clearly does not meet all three. For example, one group could develop a study of a job seeker who had reasonably good training for the job sought but who dressed very poorly for the interview and arrived 20 minutes late. Other groups could work out combinations, perhaps as defined by you. Perhaps all hypothetical job seekers could be seeking the same type of job. Have each group role-play an interview involving their job seeker and an employer. When all the interviews have been completed, all present get to vote on whom they'd hire.
- Prepare in advance case studies of job seekers, each of whom has deficits in one area of an employer's expectations. Present the case studies in oral or written form. Each small group is to decide whom they would hire. All groups might then present their conclusions in a discussion involving the entire group.
- Discuss the "right" way to dress and groom for a contact with a prospective employer. Everyone has an opinion on this. Mine is as follows: Dress and groom like the person to whom you would expect to report. Don't overdress. If you want a job as a mechanic, dress clothing is not appropriate. Stress that personal cleanliness is a must for those applying for any job.

DISCUSSION/QUIZ QUESTIONS

Employer Expectations

1. What are the major areas an employer will use to evaluate you for a position? Why is each of these important?
2. What are the three types of skills that make up the personal skills triangle? Give examples of each.
3. How should you dress for an interview?
4. Name as many factors involved in your personal appearance as possible.
5. Other than previous jobs, name other sources to support your transferable skills.
6. Which type of skills is not mentioned in the interview by most job seekers? Why would an employer need to know about these?
7. Name the three things that make you a good employee. For each of these, tell what type of skill is involved.
8. What sorts of problems would a person who did not have a clear job objective have in convincing an employer to hire him or her?
9. Based on the interview, could a person with less experience be hired instead of a more experienced person? Why?
10. Name the three things that would be most important to you if you were an employer selecting a new employee. Why are these factors important?

CHAPTER TWO

The DataTrakt®
A Pocket Full of Power

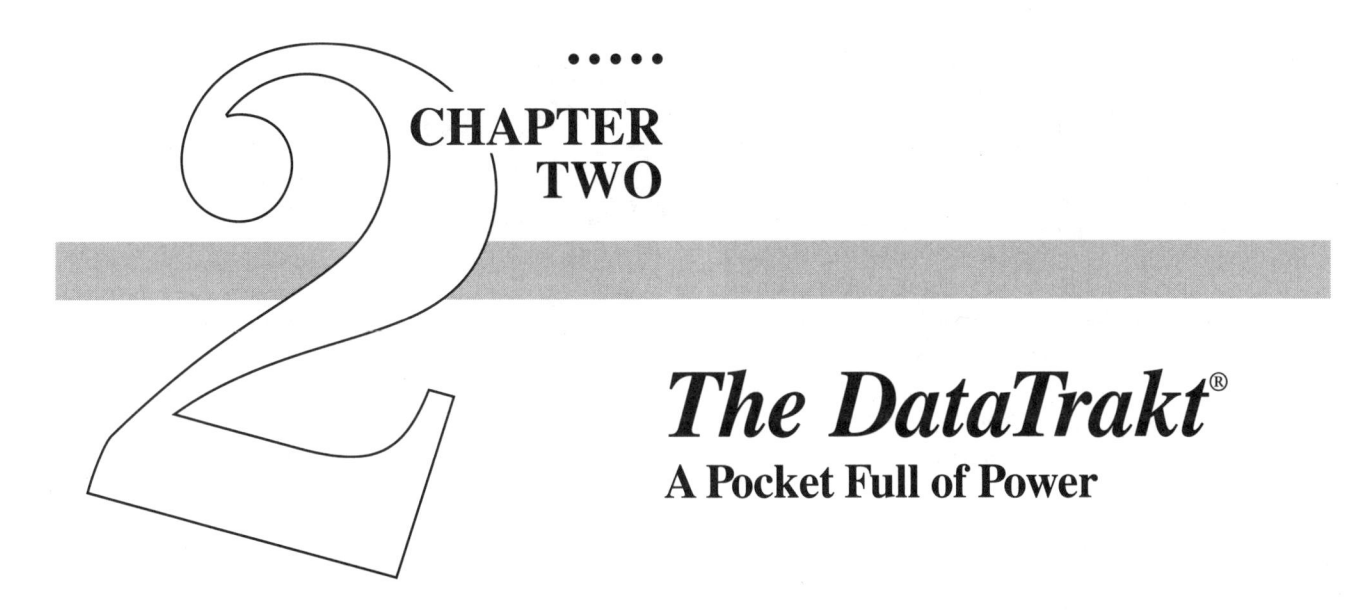

The DataTrakt is a job-search tool that was developed in response to a need. Most job seekers simply do not have memory recall of the details required on most applications. The DataTrakt provides these details. The DataTrakt also provides a baseline of information that most job seekers need to gather and review prior to the job search itself. Carrying the DataTrakt with them may permit even poor readers to retrieve critical information and complete most applications accurately.

Because the DataTrakt is brief and is oriented towards the collection of information, the core exercise requires the accurate completion of all entries. With job seekers who have very limited or no previous work experience, this may not be as simple as it seems.

CORE EXERCISE

Completing the DataTrakt

Objective/Rationale

You can do this core exercise in the class or workshop following the assignment of *The Work Book* chapter as homework. Completing the DataTrakt as a group exercise is quite simple. Do a quick overview of why the information is needed. Then discuss the information needed on an item-by-item basis. This procedure may be the most effective when your class or workshop is made up of youth who have had no previous work experience or persons who have limited reading skills.

Procedure

Pass along to the group the following tips regarding various items in the DataTrakt booklet. Note, however, that not all sections of the DataTrakt are covered. Also, some of the information may not relate to your job seekers.

Name Avoid nicknames here.

Social Security Number If you are dealing with immigrants or others not likely to have social security numbers, familiarize yourself with the local procedures for obtaining them and explain those procedures thoroughly. As part of your class, you might also have your people visit a social security office and/or fill out an application for a number.

Address Explain that the address to list is the one at which the job seeker can be reached by mail.

Phone Numbers If your job seekers do not have necessary numbers now, tell them to get the information as soon as possible.

Work Experience The mere presence of this section assumes that the job seeker has had some work experience. Part-time jobs, summer jobs, and family business activities can all be listed here—even if they were held for short periods of time. Some people may have had considerable volunteer or military experience. Ask students to refer to them. In order to accurately complete the sections Types of Data/Information Used, People-Oriented Duties/Responsibilities, Types of Things Used on the Job, Creative Ideas, and Other Duties and Special Responsibilities, the job seeker may have to think long and hard. The effort expended here can pay dividends, however, as these items form the basis for subsequent interview responses and other tasks.

Education and Training Consult *The Work Book* for examples.

Job-Related Personal Information As this section was detailed in *The Work Book,* it should present few problems. Some of your people may have some difficulty dealing with vocational assessment issues such as Position Desired, Transferable Skills, and Self-Management Skills. As indicated in *The Work Book* Introduction, it is necessary to have a job objective before beginning a job search. What if some job seekers do not have a job objective? They will need to establish such an objective—even a tentative one—before proceeding.

References Besides getting the necessary data, your job seekers may also need help in identifying who would be a good reference for them. Discussion might help clarify the issue.

Questions to Ask Employers/Callback Closing/Proof-by-Example Sections These are all to be completed at a later time. Information and instructions may be found in the appropriate chapters of *The Work Book.*

You can also assign the completion of the DataTrakt as homework. Before making the assignment, you should give these guidelines:

- Use a pencil.
- Obtain the exact data requested.
- Don't complete the last two pages.
- Jot down all questions or problem areas for later review.

Review the completed DataTrakts in class. As the DataTrakts are reviewed, the questions and problem areas raised by the job seekers should form the basis of a useful discussion. Refer to the comments earlier in this section for tips on completing various items. To assure that the group has a clear understanding of what is desired, I suggest you discuss each item of the DataTrakt beginning with Name.

DATATRAKT EXERCISE

Getting References

Objective/Rationale

In this exercise job seekers are to personally contact people they may want to use as references and to verify the nature of information that would be given to a prospective employer.

Procedure

Step 1: Have the job seekers make a list of everyone they could possibly use as a reference. See Chapter 2 of *The Work Book* for suggested sources. Each person's list should have at least 15 names on it.

Step 2: Have the job seekers mark those references who would be the best ones from a prospective employer's point of view (provided a positive reference were given, of course). Before the best references are indicated, it may be wise for the students to break up into groups of three or four so that the issue can be discussed. The groups might want to answer questions such as, "Would an aunt be a better reference than a previous employer?" Each job seeker would choose the four or five best prospects.

DATATRAKT EXERCISE

Researching Previous Experience

Objective/Rationale

The sections of the DataTrakt that require Types of Data/Information Used, People-Oriented Duties/Responsibilities, Types of Things Used on the Job, Creative Ideas, and Other Duties and Special Responsibilities may need to be researched. Memory will be enough for many people, but too often major tasks are overlooked. Two very good resources to review regarding the duties of any previous job are *The Dictionary of Occupational Titles* and *The Occupational Outlook Handbook.* (Both are published by the U.S. Department of Labor and are available at most public libraries.) Additional titles are listed in the Annotated Bibliography beginning on page 45 under Career Information Books.

DISCUSSION/QUIZ QUESTIONS

The Datatrakt

1. What did you learn about yourself in completing the DataTrakt?
2. What have you learned that will be most helpful to you in an interview?
3. Name three methods of handling a job gap in listing work experience.
4. List at least five ways the DataTrakt can be used to help you in your job search.
5. What sections of your background were the weakest in supporting your job objective? What other things that you did can you use to overcome this weakness?
6. How can life experiences be used to support your job objective even if you were not paid for them? Give at least three examples of life experiences you have had that can be used to support your job objective.
7. What is the difference between duties and responsibilities in listing your experience? Give examples for both from your DataTrakt.
8. What sort of people make the best references for you to use?
9. What steps should you take before using anyone as a reference?
10. List at least three accomplishments you can use to support your ability to do the job you want. At least two of them should be from situations other than work.

CHAPTER THREE

Applications
Screening Yourself into the Running

Applications are most often used by personnel offices (especially those in large companies). Smaller companies often don't use them at all. Many books on job seeking overemphasize the importance of applications. Don't misunderstand—they are used to screen people in and out of interviews. But, they shouldn't be considered as primary interview-getting devices.

Chapter 3 of *The Work Book* puts applications into their proper perspective. An application form structures most of the questions asked in a job interview and thus provides a very useful tool for identifying problem areas that a job seeker is likely to encounter in face-to-face contacts with employers. For example, by knowing how to explain an employment gap on an application, job seekers learn how to handle that issue in an interview.

CORE EXERCISE

Applications

Objective/Rationale

This group exercise is most effective if done *before* the chapter has been completed. Give no warning. In the exercise the job seekers are asked to complete an application as if it were a real one. On pages 10–11, I have included a sample of an application (actually a composite of those used by various companies). It contains entries that touch upon difficult or controversial areas. Reproduce copies of this sample application for your class members.

Procedure

Step 1: Tell your students you want each of them to complete an application as if it were a real one. Do this very matter-of-factly, and don't provide any more instructions or comments.

Step 2: Pass out copies of the sample application in this guide or some you have selected from local sources. Don't give out any that are too long or complex.

Step 3: Allow enough time for most of the group to complete the application. Since it's not critical that everyone finish together, simply ask slow writers to go on to step 4 after they have finished.

Step 4: Have the students exchange their completed applications with each other.

Step 5: Now everyone should review the application just received. The reviewer is to assume the role of the employer. Any entries that create a negative impression should be circled. The following are among the points to be considered: Is the application neat? Is it complete? What about spelling? Did the applicant follow all instructions? Is there any information that could be interpreted negatively (unexplained job gaps, for example)? Allow about 5–10 minutes for the review.

Step 6: Initiate a discussion. What impressions did the applications make? What errors were found? Would the reviewers have interviewed the

APPLICATION FOR EMPLOYMENT
(Please print using a pen or type.)

Name _____
       Last   First   Middle initial

Present address _____
                 Street   City   State   ZIP code

Permanent address _____
                   Street   City   State   ZIP code

Phone number (_____) _____   Soc. sec. no. _____-_____-_____

Position desired _____   Salary desired _____

EXPERIENCE (Furnish record of past employment/unemployment, beginning with present or most recent position and working backwards.)

From (Mo./yr.)	Name of firm	Start salary	Last position	Duties performed
	Address			
To (Mo./yr.)		End salary	Reason for leaving	
	Supervisor Phone			
From (Mo./yr.)	Name of firm	Start salary	Last position	Duties performed
	Address			
To (Mo./yr.)		End salary	Reason for leaving	
	Supervisor Phone			
From (Mo./yr.)	Name of firm	Start salary	Last position	Duties performed
	Address			
To (Mo./yr.)		End salary	Reason for leaving	
	Supervisor Phone			
From (Mo./yr.)	Name of firm	Start salary	Last position	Duties performed
	Address			
To (Mo./yr.)		End salary	Reason for leaving	
	Supervisor Phone			

AVAILABILITY

Date available _____   Circle days available. Su M T W Th F S   Hours available _____

Available for overtime?   ☐ Yes ☐ No   Willing to relocate?   ☐ Yes ☐ No

Can you complete an Employment Eligibility Verification (Form I-9) as required by the INS?   ☐ Yes ☐ No

Do you have any condition(s) that may limit your ability to perform the essential functions of the job you are seeking?   ☐ Yes ☐ No

If yes, explain. _____
_____

Have you ever been convicted of a crime other than a minor traffic violation?   ☐ Yes ☐ No

If yes: Name crime(s). _____

List date(s) and place(s). _____
_____

EDUCATION

High School
- Name _____
- Address _____

Did you graduate? ☐ Yes ☐ No
If no, circle last year. 1 2 3 4
Major courses _____

College
- Name _____
- Address _____

Did you graduate? ☐ Yes ☐ No
If no, circle last year. 1 2 3 4
Major courses _____

Other
- Name _____
- Address _____

Course description _____
Dates attended _____
Diploma _____ Certificate _____

Do you have any trade/professional licenses or certifications? ☐ Yes ☐ No
If yes, specify:

Type _____ Issuing authority _____ Exp. date _____

Describe any other training, skills, or interests that especially qualify you for the position for which you are applying.

_____
_____

REFERENCES
(List two people you have known for at least three years who are not relatives or former employers.)

Name	Address	Phone	Occupation

Do not write below this line.

OFFICE USE ONLY (post-hire)

Hire date: _____ Position _____ Rate _____

Employee no. _____ Check one: FT ☐ PT ☐ T ☐ S ☐

Gender:
☐ Female
☐ Male

Marital Status:
☐ Married
☐ Single

Race/ethnicity:
☐ White   ☐ Black   ☐ Hispanic
☐ Asian   ☐ American Indian

Date of birth: _____   Work permit: ☐ Yes ☐ No

Chapter 3   Applications   11

applicants or not? Ask any additional questions that would elicit the job seekers' new perceptions regarding the importance of applications.

Step 7: Collect the applications and use them for future reference. You could also return them to the original writers. (If you plan to do step 9, gather up the applications after the writers have had the chance to examine them.)

Step 8: Assign as homework Chapter 3 of *The Work Book*.

Step 9: Following completion of Chapter 3, distribute new copies of the same application you handed out in step 2. Either in class or as homework, have everyone fill out the application again. Ask the people how they improved. If they can't answer, pass out the earlier applications for comparison.

APPLICATIONS EXERCISE

Using Your "Wrong" Hand

Objective/Rationale

The idea here is to create an application that has a very poor appearance.

Procedure

Step 1: Select a part of a blank application form for participants to complete. Instruct right-handed people to write with the left hand and left-handed people to write with the right hand.

Step 2: Be certain to allow enough time for everyone to become frustrated. It's okay if they don't finish.

Step 3: Have everyone exchange applications.

Step 4: Ask each person to evaluate the application received as if he or she were an employer. Ask several of the participants the following questions: "Would you screen out this application?" "Why?" "What assumptions do you make about the person who completed this application?"

Step 5: Point out that an application does not present applicants as they are. Mention that applications are often used to screen applicants out rather than in. Also, point out the importance of appearance, one of an employer's major expectations.

APPLICATIONS EXERCISE

Gathering Applications

Objective/Rationale

This is a field exercise that requires job seekers to go out and collect applications. This exercise has two purposes. It makes applicants less fearful of meeting real employers. It also demonstrates the limitations of applications as job-finding tools.

Procedure

Step 1: By a designated target time or date, everyone is to collect as many different applications as possible (at least three each). Applications may be obtained from any source. Participants are not to look for a job at this point; they are just to collect applications.

Step 2: In a subsequent class or session, review what happened. Ask: "Was it hard?" "Did anyone get a job offer?" "With whom did you speak?"

Step 3: There are several points likely to be made:
- Some (many?) small business do not even use applications.
- Job seekers can speak directly to employers, even without an application.
- Applications have very little to do with getting interviews.

Step 4: Encourage students to return the completed applications to their sources if they wish. Applications can also be "filed" for future reference.

APPLICATIONS EXERCISE

Screening for Negatives

Objective/Rationale

Applications completed by each job seeker will be reviewed by others who will look for any entry that makes a negative impression.

Procedure

Step 1: After all the assignments in Chapter 3 of *The Work Book* have been completed, ask each job seeker to complete an application.

Step 2: Everyone's completed application is to be reviewed by someone else.

Step 3: Everyone is now to evaluate carefully the application they have as if they were an employer. Is it neat? Are there any errors? Does anything said make a negative impression? Ask participants to mark any problem areas. If they have problems doing this, you may wish to review the applications after the student reviewers have finished.

Step 4: Return the corrected copies to their original writers.

Step 5: Discuss what was found.

APPLICATIONS EXERCISE
Discussion on the Morality of Telling the "Truth"

Objective/Rationale

In *The Work Book* job seekers are encouraged to tell the truth. But they are also encouraged to present themselves in a positive way and not provide unrequested negative information. For example, a person who has been convicted of a felony may be advised to leave that part of an application blank and explain the omission in an interview. Is that morally right? Should the situation be handled differently?

These issues will invariably come up when dealing with applications. The wording chosen for dealing with the issue was carefully selected but may not resolve everyone's need for a universally applicable answer.

The morality issue is a complicated one that each person will ultimately have to decide for him- or herself. My own preference, evidenced in *The Work Book* with such issues as job gaps, is to tell the truth in the best possible light.

Procedure

I suggest you consider structuring a discussion on the morality of the issue, basing the discussion on specific examples that are difficult to resolve. Perhaps assigning two groups to argue opposing views would be useful. Allow them just a few minutes to prepare.

APPLICATIONS EXERCISE
Albert C. Smith (#1)

Objective/Rationale

This exercise is best done *after* the job seekers have done Chapter 3 in *The Work Book*. This guide contains two examples of an application completed by a fictitious Albert C. Smith. In the first one (pages 14–15) Albert has done almost everything incorrectly. The second example (pages 16–17) fixes most of his errors. This exercise can be fun. You may also wish to put together your own version of Albert's application. If so, use examples related to your job seekers.

Procedure

Step 1: Distribute copies of Albert's poor application.

Step 2: Have everyone go through and mark any error they can find on the application.

Step 3: (Optional) Divide people into groups of no more than five or six people each. Have a contest to see which group finds the most errors.

Step 4: Have everyone count up the number of errors found.

Step 5: The person (or group) with the highest number now reviews each error found, by section. Overlooked errors can then be pointed out by the others.

Step 6: Distribute copies of Albert's good application. (This could have been done prior to step 5.)

APPLICATIONS EXERCISE
Albert C. Smith (#2)

Goals

- To have students identify both major and minor flaws in Albert C. Smith's application and to explain why the flaws are flaws.
- To have students correct the poor application and compare it to the good application.
- To have students pick out the problems that remain on the good A. C. Smith application.
- To reinforce the concept of applications as presented in *The Work Book*.

# SEARS
APPLICATION FOR EMPLOYMENT
(PLEASE PRINT REQUESTED INFORMATION IN INK.)

Date: *Apr. 9*

Sears is an Equal Opportunity Employer and does not discriminate against any individual in any phase of employment in accordance with the requirements of local, state, and federal law. In addition, Sears has adopted an Affirmative Action Program with the goal of ensuring equitable representation of qualified women, minorities, Vietnam Era and disabled veterans, and other disabled individuals, at all job levels.

Applicants may be subject to testing for illegal drugs. In addition, applicants for certain positions that receive a conditional offer of employment must pass a medical examination prior to receiving a confirmed offer of employment.

This application will be considered active for 60 days. If you have not been employed within this period and are still interested in employment at Sears, please contact the office where you applied and request that your application be reactivated.

PERSONAL INFORMATION

Last Name	First Name	Middle Name	Social Security No.
Albert	C.	Smith	411-~~26~~ 76 -2614

Street Address	City	State	Zip Code	County	Telephone No.
1531 N. Otter					(949) 1430

If hired, can you furnish proof of age? ☒ Yes ☐ No

If hired, can you furnish proof that you are legally entitled to work in the U.S.? ☒ Yes ☐ No

Answer the following questions only if the position for which you are applying requires driving.

Are you licensed to drive a car? ☐ Yes ☒ No   Is license valid in this state? ☐ Yes ☐ No

Have you ever been employed by Sears or a subsidiary of Sears? ☐ Yes ☒ No
If Yes, note unit number and address | Termination Date | Position

Do you have any relatives employed by Sears in the store or unit in which you are applying? ☒ Yes ☐ No   If Yes, Name/Relationship: *Vickie Sims Cosine*

In order to assure proper placement of all associates, please list any special skills, training, or experiences which qualify you for the position for which you are applying.

~~~~~~~~~~~~~~~~~~~~~~~~

AVAILABILITY

I am applying for the following position:
☒ Sales ☒ Office ☒ Mechanical ☒ Merchandise Handling
☒ Other (specify): *Anything*

Date you are available to start work: *ASAP*

I am seeking (check only one):
☒ Inventory/Special Projects (6 days or less)
☒ Seasonal employment (one season, e.g., Christmas)
☒ Regular employment (employ. for indefinite per. of time)

I am available for:
☒ Part-time employment ☒ Full-time employment
Complete the Hours Available For Work Chart below.

If temporary, indicate dates available: *ASAP*

Total hours available per week: *40+*

	Sun.	Mon.	Tues.	Wed.	Thurs.	Fri.	Sat.
FROM		*Anytime*					
TO							

MISCELLANEOUS

Within the past seven years, have you been convicted of a crime involving dishonesty or violence? (A conviction record will not necessarily be a bar to employment.)
☒ Yes ☒ No
If Yes, explain: ~~drunk in public~~

10534 Rev. 7/92

EDUCATION

Names and Locations of Schools Attended	Did you graduate? YES	NO	Courses of Study		
High School: Crestview Jr. High, Scranton PA	Yes		General		
College: Warren Central SH	"		Major: College Prep		Degree
Other (Name and type): IUPUI	"		(undecided)		—

WORK EXPERIENCE

List below your four most recent employers, starting with your present or last employer. List under company name any periods of unemployment. If you were employed under another name, please enter under the company name.

Company Name	Address & Phone	Mo./Yr.	Rate of Pay	Title of Job Held / Name of Supervisor	Reason for Leaving
Fred Wills	?	From 7/94 To 10/94	Starting 4.25 Final "	Helper/Labor / Rafael	Boss picked on me
KPS	Walnut St, Indpls. Ind.	From ?/92 To	Starting 1/94 Final	Clean up / Eric Burgess	Fired
Wayne Constr (1430 N Andersen, Indpls. Ind.)	→	From 1989 To 3.25 (switch)	Starting 1992 Final 4.10	Jackhammer oper./wiring / Mark Lenski	Co. went broke
Central State Mental Hosp.	Washington St, Indpls.	From 1988 To 1989	Starting $2 hr Final "	clean-up / Lynn Donovan	I got better & was discharged

PLEASE READ THE FOLLOWING PARAGRAPH BEFORE SIGNING THIS APPLICATION

I certify that the information contained in this application is correct to the best of my knowledge and understand that any misstatement or omission of information is grounds for dismissal in accordance with Sears, Roebuck and Co. policy. I authorize the references listed above to give you any and all information concerning my previous employment and any pertinent information they may have, personal or otherwise, and release all parties from all liability for any damage that may result from furnishing same to you. In consideration of my employment, I agree to conform to the rules and regulations of Sears, Roebuck and Co., and my employment and compensation can be terminated with or without cause, and with or without notice, at any time, at the option of either the Company or myself. I understand that no unit manager or representative of Sears, Roebuck and Co. other than an Officer of the Company, has any authority to enter into any agreement for employment for any specified period of time, or to make any agreement contrary to the foregoing. In some states, the law requires that Sears have my written permission before obtaining consumer reports on me, and I hereby authorize Sears to obtain such reports.

Applicant's Signature: Al Smith   Date: 4-9

OFFICE USE ONLY

Unit Name and Number			
Employment Date: ASAP	Dept. or Div. No.		✓ REGULAR ✓ PART-TIME
Job Title	Job Code	Job Grade	
Compensation Arrangement	Associate No.	Timecard Rack No.	
Authorized Signature: Al Smith		Date: 4-9	

10534 Rev. 7/92 Backer

Chapter 3 Applications

SEARS
APPLICATION FOR EMPLOYMENT
(PLEASE PRINT REQUESTED INFORMATION IN INK.)

Date: 4-9-94

Sears is an Equal Opportunity Employer and does not discriminate against any individual in any phase of employment in accordance with the requirements of local, state, and federal law. In addition, Sears has adopted an Affirmative Action Program with the goal of ensuring equitable representation of qualified women, minorities, Vietnam Era and disabled veterans, and other disabled individuals, at all job levels.

Applicants may be subject to testing for illegal drugs. In addition, applicants for certain positions that receive a conditional offer of employment must pass a medical examination prior to receiving a confirmed offer of employment.

This application will be considered active for 60 days. If you have not been employed within this period and are still interested in employment at Sears, please contact the office where you applied and request that your application be reactivated.

PERSONAL INFORMATION

Last Name	First Name	Middle Name	Social Security No.
Smith	Albert	Charles	411-76-2614

Street Address	City	State	Zip Code	County	Telephone No.
1531 N. Otter St.	Scranton	PA	18602	Marion	(717) 949-1430

If hired, can you furnish proof of age? ☑ Yes ☐ No

If hired, can you furnish proof that you are legally entitled to work in the U.S.? ☑ Yes ☐ No

Answer the following questions only if the position for which you are applying requires driving.

Are you licensed to drive a car? ☐ Yes ☑ No   Is license valid in this state? ☐ Yes ☐ No

Have you ever been employed by Sears or a subsidiary of Sears? ☐ Yes ☑ No

If Yes, note unit number and address: —   Termination Date: —   Position: —

Do you have any relatives employed by Sears in the store or unit in which you are applying? ☑ Yes ☐ No   If Yes, Name/Relationship: Vickie Sims/Cousin

In order to assure proper placement of all associates, please list any special skills, training, or experiences which qualify you for the position for which you are applying.

(1.) Attended and successfully completed course of study, U.S. Air Force Radio Repair Training School. (2.) Served as Big Brother through affiliation with National Association of Electronic Salespeople.

AVAILABILITY

I am applying for the following position:
☑ Sales ☐ Office ☐ Mechanical ☐ Merchandise Handling
☑ Other (specify): Repair (both in home electronics)

Date you are available to start work: _____

I am seeking (check only one):
☐ Inventory/Special Projects (6 days or less)
☐ Seasonal employment (one season, e.g., Christmas)
☑ Regular employment (employ. for indefinite per. of time)

I am available for:
☐ Part-time employment ☑ Full-time employment
Complete the Hours Available For Work Chart below.

If temporary, indicate dates available: —

Total hours available per week: —

	Sun.	Mon.	Tues.	Wed.	Thurs.	Fri.	Sat.
FROM	8a.m.	8a.m.	8a.m.	8a.m.	8a.m.	8a.m.	8a.m.
TO	close	close	close	close	close	close	close

MISCELLANEOUS

Within the past seven years, have you been convicted of a crime involving dishonesty or violence? (A conviction record will not necessarily be a bar to employment.)
☐ Yes ☑ No

If Yes, explain: _____

10534 Rev. 7/92

16   The Work Book   Instructor's Guide

EDUCATION

Names and Locations of Schools Attended	Did you graduate? YES / NO	Courses of Study
High School Warren Central H.S., Scranton, PA	✓	College Preparatory
College Indiana – Purdue Univ. at Indianapolis, IN		Major: Electronics Degree: (In progress)
Other (Name and type) —	— —	—

WORK EXPERIENCE

List below your four most recent employers, starting with your present or last employer. List under company name any periods of unemployment. If you were employed under another name, please enter under the company name.

Company Name	Address & Phone	Mo. / Yr.	Rate of Pay	Title of Job Held / Name of Supervisor	Reason for Leaving
Fred Wills, Electrician (After 5 months, college courses)	1275 E. 11th St. Indianapolis, IN 46156 (317) 555-2121	From 7-94 To 10-94	Starting $4.25/hr. Final $4.25/hr.	Electrician's Helper / Rafael Castillo	Work slowdown, limited schedule.
Indianapolis Public Schools	5300 Walnut St. Indianapolis, IN 47232 (317) 555-3131	From 9-92 To 1-94	Starting $3.90/hr. Final $4.10/hr.	Custodian / Eric Borgess	Desired a more demanding position.
Wayne Construction	1436 N. Anderson Dr. Indianapolis, IN 48139 (317) 555-4141	From 7-89 To 8-92	Starting $3.30/hr. Final $3.75/hr.	Electrical Equip. Installer / Mark Lenski	Company went out of business.
—	—	From — To —	Starting — Final —	—	—

PLEASE READ THE FOLLOWING PARAGRAPH BEFORE SIGNING THIS APPLICATION

I certify that the information contained in this application is correct to the best of my knowledge and understand that any misstatement or omission of information is grounds for dismissal in accordance with Sears, Roebuck and Co. policy. I authorize the references listed above to give you any and all information concerning my previous employment and any pertinent information they may have, personal or otherwise, and release all parties from all liability for any damage that may result from furnishing same to you. In consideration of my employment, I agree to conform to the rules and regulations of Sears, Roebuck and Co., and my employment and compensation can be terminated with or without cause, and with or without notice, at any time, at the option of either the Company or myself. I understand that no unit manager or representative of Sears, Roebuck and Co. other than an Officer of the Company, has any authority to enter into any agreement for employment for any specified period of time, or to make any agreement contrary to the foregoing. In some states, the law requires that Sears have my written permission before obtaining consumer reports on me, and I hereby authorize Sears to obtain such reports.

Applicant's Signature: *Albert C. Smith*   Date: 4-9-94

OFFICE USE ONLY

Unit Name and Number			
Employment Date	Dept. or Div. No.		☐ REGULAR ☐ PART-TIME
Job Title	Job Code	Job Grade	
Compensation Arrangement	Associate No.	Timecard Rack No.	
Authorized Signature		Date	

10534 Rev. 7/92 Backer

Materials
- A. C. Smith applications
- Pencils

Procedure

Step 1: Divide the students into groups of three, and give each person a copy of A. C. Smith's bad application.

Step 2: Allow the groups two minutes of scanning time.

Step 3: Ask the whole group to identify glaring flaws (1–2 minutes).

Step 4: Tell the entire group that there are over 50 flaws on Albert's application and that each small group is to identify as many errors as possible in ten minutes.

Step 5: After ten minutes, have each group present the errors it found. This might be done by a group leader. The leader should explain the group's reasoning and give suggestions as to how Albert might improve the application.

Step 6: Review the bad A. C. Smith application yourself, proceeding line by line. Missed flaws and possible corrections should be discussed.

Step 7: Pass out the good A. C. Smith application and ask the group to compare the two versions.

Step 8: Tell the group there are still some mistakes. See if they can find them quickly.

Step 9: Query the group as to why the good application is more acceptable.

Step 10: Have students complete Chapter 3 of *The Work Book*. For homework, assign the application that appears at the end of that chapter.

Step 11: In the next class, have students review each others' applications. Address problems as they arise.

Step 12: Review each application for accuracy and critique as needed.

DISCUSSION/QUIZ QUESTIONS

Applications

1. Name the major sections or types of information on most applications.
2. Is completing applications a good way to find a job? Why?
3. Are there better ways to find job openings? If so, name some and explain why they are better.
4. What is the first thing you do before you begin to fill out an application? What sorts of things do you need to watch for?
5. What can you do if an application asks you a question that, if you answer it honestly, might get you rejected from consideration?
6. If you lie on an application, would the employer be justified in firing you later if he or she found out? Why or why not?
7. Name a few questions not asked on most applications because of antidiscrimination laws. Are there situations when you—if you were the employer—would want to know the facts on one or more of these questions before making a decision to hire? Describe those situations.
8. Many applications have sections that don't get completely filled in. What can you often do with this blank space?
9. Do all businesses use applications to screen employees? Explain.
10. Why do many businesses use applications? Give at least two reasons.

CHAPTER FOUR

JIST Cards
A Taste of Your Talents

The best rationale for the JIST card is to define a hypothetical situation and the standard method used to handle that situation.

Situation #1: A 19-year-old girl is looking for her first job as a cashier. She has had some training in high school and two months of experience at the state-fair ticket booth. The applications she fills out list only one job as experience.

Situation #2: A Ph.D. candidate is looking for a job as a teacher at a junior college. She has a four-page resume of publications and a variety of work experience. Some of the work experiences are relevant, others are marginal.

These situations are very different on the surface, but they have a similar problem: how can the applicants quickly communicate to a prospective employer that they have something to offer? On one hand, a semiblank application form showing two months of experience is not impressive. On the other hand, a four-page resume is anything but clear, succinct, and to the point.

The JIST card, in spite of its small size (or perhaps because of it), is a very sophisticated tool. It bypasses all the irrelevant barriers to clear communication and gets right to the essence of what an employer wants to know and a job seeker needs to express.

For the 19-year-old, the problem of limited experience can be compensated for by clarity of objective, enthusiasm, and willingness to work. Where an application or a traditional resume does not do her justice, a 3" x 5" card can.

For the Ph.D. candidate with all the publications, the JIST card forces her to make a clear statement of objective and to justify it succinctly. A well-done JIST card presents the *essence* of what an employer needs to know. It is a truthful, positive, and precise statement of a job seeker's abilities, skills, and objectives. And because of its brevity and careful construction, it communicates the required information far more rapidly than other job-search tools, such as applications or resumes.

The JIST card also provides a brief, positive self-statement that will be repeated many times in various ways. This drill will help the job seeker prepare for unexpected situations that may arise during job interviews. Since all the information on the JIST card should be honest and positive, it will often help provide the job seeker with a sense of self-confidence.

Please note that the JIST card is a very effective job-search tool. If at all possible, see that all students or participants have a number of their final cards printed for distribution to employers.

CORE EXERCISE

JIST Card

Objective/Rationale

In this exercise, use a large chalkboard or flip chart to complete a sample JIST card for one of the students or workshop participants. This is best done prior to assigning the DataTrakt chapter of *The Work Book*.

Step 1: Explain the basics of what a JIST card is and how it will be used. It is best to have sample copies available. Use the samples that follow this exercise if no others are available, or refer to the appropriate pages in *The Work Book*.

Step 2: Section by section, on a flip chart, construct a sample of a JIST card's content. Explain as you go. Use as an example the job objective and related information of someone in the group.

Step 3: When done, ask everyone for feedback. Does the card communicate the essentials? Does it impress?

Step 4: Have everyone draft a card using the same basic format. Help individuals as needed.

Step 5: If time permits, have everyone read his or her card aloud. Ask for feedback and make specific suggestions, as needed. Provide ample positive feedback. Encourage everyone to make improvements as needed.

Robert Sherry Home (306) 443-1776
　　　　　　　　　　Messages (306) 443-3467

Position Desired　　　　　　　　General Laborer

Skills: Over 12 years experience as general laborer in construction. Can use all hand and power tools, mix mortar and cement, carry building materials and build scaffolding. Can do roofing, dry wall and painting. Willing to learn and a hard worker.

Guarantee highest quality job.

Strong, Prompt and Dependable

PAMELA PRICE　　　Messages (215) 556-9769
　　　　　　　　　　　　　　　　　221-8880

Position Desired: Nurse-Aide

Skills: One year experience in the field of Nurse-Aide. Can take temperature, blood pressure, pulse, intake/output on patients, put patients on the bedpan, work a wheelchair, bathe patients, dress them, and make beds. Love helping others.

Work well under supervision.

Prompt, dependable, great attendance, quick learner.

Joyce Wong　　　　　　　　　　(501) 695-7413 (H)
　　　　　　　　　　　　　　　　(501) 695-3576 (M)

Position Desired:　　　　　　　Cashier/Clerk

Skills: Four years experience as cashier and clerk. Can operate cash register accurately, prepare counters, process supply request forms, stock shelves, and set up goods for sale. Can sort and keep accurate logs of registered mail.

Punctual, with excellent attendance record.

Hardworking　　　Reliable　　　Pleasant

Phillip Taylor　　　　　　　　Home: (807) 237-9653
　　　　　　　　　　　　　　　Work: (807) 237-5662

Position Desired:　　Building/Maintenance Manager

Skills: Over 20 years performing and supervising all aspects of building maintenance, plumbing, electricity, heating/cooling systems, and housekeeping. Have supervised up to 60 employees. Able to perform record keeping.

Willing to work weekends and holidays.

Reliable, self-starter, and problem solver.

SHARON ROOD　　　*Messages: (512) 391-7134*

Position Desired: Seamstress

Skills: Over 4 years experience in sewing. Can do hems, seams, pockets, zippers, linings, cuffs, buttonholes, waistbands, pleats, elastic, and flaps. Can preshrink materials, pin patterns, and take measurements. Have experience in alterations. Worked with variety of fabrics such as polyester, wool, and denim.

Produce top quality work.

Accurate, Willing to Learn, Dependable

MARTA GAIZA　　　　　　**(714) 896-5600 (H)**
　　　　　　　　　　　　　　(714) 896-2611 (M)

Position Desired:　File Clerk and Receptionist

Skills: Nine months experience performing general office duties. Can file, answer phone, take messages, and operate a 15-line switchboard. Can operate photocopier and adding machine, and maintain a business log.

Willing to work overtime to meet employer's needs.

Good with People. Neat Appearance. Pleasant Speaking Voice.

JIST CARD EXERCISE

Constructing Cards in Pairs

Objective/Rationale

While JIST cards appear to be simple, many people do not have the writing or other skills needed to do them without help. Constructing good JIST cards is something of an art. In almost every group, though, some people will show a real talent for putting them together. This exercise puts those people to work helping others. I use this sort of approach often in groups and am very aware of how the helpers gain as much as those being helped. The approach also builds group cohesion and allows you to give the benefit of your expertise to the one or two in every group who truly need you.

Step 1: After everyone in the group has been introduced to JIST cards and has had a chance to put together a rough draft of one (as either a homework assignment or an earlier exercise), explain that they will now try to improve their work.

Step 2: Ask everyone to get into pairs.

Step 3: Ask if there is anyone in the group who had a problem in coming up with a good job objective. Use your own and the group's knowledge to solve this problem. Then ask for and resolve several other problems that people experienced. This establishes a problem-solving mode as well as gives a few models for improving cards.

Step 4: Have partners go over their cards with each other section by section. Encourage each partner to help make the other's card presentation as positive as possible.

Step 5: Notice which pairs are working well together and which ones do not seem to have the skills to improve their cards. As the more able pairs are finishing—but before their own cards are "perfect"—quietly ask one or both members to go over and help someone who is having trouble. Tell the helpers how good their cards are, make a few suggestions, and move them. Be sensitive to the group members having problems, and do not draw attention to what you are doing.

Step 6: Keep circulating through the pairs, and keep everyone as productive as possible. Give constructive suggestions and compliments. It is often more important for people to feel confident in what they have (if it is honest and "good enough") than to overimprove it.

Step 7: Spend personal time where it is needed most. This could mean with someone who really requires individual and expert help in constructing his or her card. If necessary, see such people after the session to give them the help they need.

Step 8: Wrap up the session when almost everyone seems finished. To allow for final rewrites, announce in advance that time is almost up. When done, ask for comments on the process from the group or questions that remain on improving their cards. Let them know that they can continue to improve their cards after the session.

Tip: Remember how small a JIST card is. Content that is too long must be edited down so that everything that remains supports the job objective. Content that is too short must be built up with meaningful additions.

JIST CARD EXERCISE

Having Cards Printed

Objective/Rationale

The JIST cards will be far more effective job-search tools if they are widely distributed. A handwritten card is better than nothing, but handwritten cards and individually typed cards require time and effort. This often results in few of them being produced and used. Solution?

Procedure

Have some printed! Having 50 cards printed at a local quick-print shop should cost under $5. The job seeker will have to supply a final, typed copy in the 3" x 5" format, although most print shops will do this as well (for a fee, of course). Perhaps you have access to a print shop in your facility. If so, I still recommend making some charge to your students. They will be more likely to use the cards if they've paid something for them.

Some of our job seekers have had their JIST cards typeset and printed with colored inks. Many of the cards have had borders or other simple graphics. Doing some of these things is more expensive than writing the cards by hand, but the extra expense and effort spent are evident in the appearance of the finished product.

DISCUSSION/QUIZ QUESTIONS

JIST Cards

1. What are the major sections of a JIST card? Why is each important?

2. Name at least four ways a JIST card can be used in your job search.

3. How could the content of a JIST card be used to help answer interview questions? Explain.

4. List the various things that can be included in your total length of experience. Use your own situation to figure your total length of experience, and give details for how you figured each component.

5. Give some advantages and disadvantages of a JIST card as compared to a resume.

6. List your three most important transferable skills (good worker traits) and give at least one good example of where you used each one on the card.

7. How many JIST cards do you think you need in your own job search? How will you use them?

8. Name a section of the JIST card that is optional. Do you plan to use this section? Why or why not?

9. Does the content of your JIST card make you feel that you are bragging? If it does, do you still think an employer should be aware of this important information about you?

10. Read your JIST card aloud to at least three people. Ask them to tell you whether they would be interested in interviewing someone like that if they were employers who had openings.

CHAPTER FIVE

Telephone Contacts
Dialing for Dollars

Chapter 5 of *The Work Book* has two primary objectives:

- to enable students to make efficient use of their time during their searches for job leads and
- to provide job seekers with structures that will enable them to make direct contact with employers.

The techniques presented in *The Work Book* have proven themselves to be extremely effective ways of helping students meet these objectives. If the methods are used well, literally hundreds of prospective employers can be contacted in one day of concentrated effort and dozens of interviews can be generated. I, however, am not advocating that job seekers make more than 20–40 calls per day.

Each job seeker's JIST card is used as a basis for developing a telephone presentation. Many of the points made in this guide regarding JIST cards will apply to telephone contacts also. Before using the JIST card as a basis for phone contacts, it is essential that the job seeker be comfortable with all that has been written on it.

The telephone contact constructed by the job seeker will provide him or her with a basic language for self-definition. Learning what to say, however, is only part of the task. As a teacher or instructor, you should see to it that the message is actually used, preferably with someone who can hire.

CORE EXERCISE #1

Telephone Contacts

Objective/Rationale
The telephone contact has both verbal and expressive dimensions. That is, the contact is learned verbally and then perfected through oral expression. In this exercise, you will introduce the concepts verbally while using a written model to supplement them.

Procedure

Step 1: Introduce the advantages of using telephone contacts for obtaining job leads. Be sure to stress the time efficiency of this method. Then, relate phone contacts to the expectations of prospective employers.

Step 2: Ask one student or participant to simply read his or her JIST card. Instruct the person to stand up and read it just as it is. When the reading has been completed, provide positive feedback.

Step 3: Now, ask the same person to remain standing and reread the JIST card. This time he or she should add, "Hello, my name is _____" and "I'm interested in a position as a(n) _____." He or she should then "smooth out" the rest of the card's content until it sounds conversational.

Step 4: Say, "Very good," or something similar. If necessary, make a few suggestions for improvement.

Step 5: Have the same person repeat the exercise. If necessary, go over and correct his or her posture. Ask the person to smile and look happy. Tell him or her to stand up and hold the JIST card so that it doesn't cover the mouth but can still be seen easily. Ask the person to make necessary changes in delivery. (It's okay to start over several times.)

Step 6: Congratulate the person! Chances are that rapid improvements were made in the quality of delivery. Ask if anyone else noticed any differences.

Step 7: Ask the group if the presentation would make a good phone contact. Would they be impressed? What is missing? Should no one have noticed, mention that a phone conversation must be closed off. The presentation needs an ending.

Step 8: Ask the same person to stand up and do the phone contact again, this time with an ending such as, "When may I come in for an interview and with whom will I be speaking?" Make a note of how many seconds the presentation took from start to finish.

Step 9: Ask, "Did anyone notice how long that took?" (Probably well under 45 seconds.) Discuss such topics as the time element, possible employer reactions, etc.

Step 10: Wrap up the exercise by telling the students that they've just learned the basics of phone contacts, and assign Chapter 5 as homework.

Option: Now or later, you could randomly ask others to read their JIST cards. Follow the same procedure as outlined above.

CORE EXERCISE #2

Telephone Contacts

Objective/Rationale

I know, there should be only one core exercise per chapter, but this activity is so good it just didn't seem right to relegate it to an "also-ran" status. As outlined, this exercise could be done before or after students have completed Chapter 5 of *The Work Book*. The exercise requires that all students get involved; everyone gets the chance to take on the role of a job seeker, a "phone answerer," and a critic. It is an enjoyable exercise where learning takes place rapidly and performance improves dramatically. Participants learn from each other and, often, everyone wins.

In this exercise students' objectives are very simple:

- to obtain an interview (even if no job opening exists now),
- to learn something, and
- to get the names of one or more persons they might speak with who may be able to help them in their job search.

Procedure

Step 1: Have the large group split up into groups of three. Encourage students to join those whom they don't know well. If your group is not a multiple of three, have the stragglers form groups of four, but no group should be larger.

Step 2: Explain the basics. Everyone in the group is to exchange roles so that each person becomes, in turn, a job seeker, a person who answers the phone, and a critic. Here is what each role involves.

- The job seeker is allowed to define the job sought, tell whom he or she is calling, and state the source of the job lead. The person is to read from either his or her JIST card or a prepared telephone script. Deviations from these procedures are to be made only as necessary.

- The phone answerer could be a receptionist, a janitor, or anyone other than an employer. The goals for the job seeker remain the same. The person who answers the phone can creatively screen out the job seeker (by transferring the call to personnel, or whatever) but shouldn't make it impossible for a job seeker to get through if a good approach is used.
- The critic listens to the exchange and says nothing until it is over. He or she should then make a special effort to provide the job seeker with feedback on how the objectives of the call could have been attained more effectively.

Step 3: Begin the exercise. Now is a good time to wander from group to group. Listen in, but avoid the temptation to say very much. Allow about 10–15 minutes for this.

Step 4: Make sure everyone plays the part of a job seeker at least once. When all have, initiate a discussion. Here are several things you could ask:
- Did anyone get past the phone answerer? If so, have the critic first explain what happened and then review the interactions as needed.
- Did anyone get turned down? Again ask the critic's opinion of what that job seeker might have done in order to have achieved at least one of the objectives. Ask the phone answerer's impressions regarding how close that job seeker came to getting through to the employer.
- Did anyone feel that a job seeker almost made it but fell short?

You probably get the idea. Encourage the group to analyze each interaction in terms of how the job seeker could more effectively meet his or her objectives.

TELEPHONE CONTACTS EXERCISE

Practice Calls to Real Employers

Objective/Rationale

While this is an exercise conducted as part of a group learning experience, it is also a serious foray into the real world of employers. In this activity students are to make actual phone calls while being monitored by their fellow group members.

Since this exercise does require access to a telephone, some modifications may have to be made. For example, in a school building you might ask students to do the exercise before or after school from a pay phone.

Procedure

Step 1: Explain the basics of the exercise and how it will be done in the environment available (the telephone situation, for example).

Step 2: Before the first call is made, help the people decide whom to call. There are several ways to do this:
- Have everyone join a small group and have each group brainstorm for possible people to call.
- Suggest that students use the Yellow Pages and their own knowledge.
- Suggest both of the above.

Step 3: At your option, you could now do one of the following:
- Have one person make a call while everyone else listens in.
- Ask the people to form groups of three or four. Each group is to elect one of its members to make a phone call. The others are to listen in.
- Make the initial call yourself. That's right. If you haven't done it yourself, how can you expect your students to do it?

Be sure to tell everyone to keep calling different places until they get to talk to someone. Remind them that people who work in small businesses will be much more accessible than those in larger ones.

Step 4: Depending on how you decided to do the exercise, you may want to review thoroughly what happened or to review the exercise lightly and encourage everyone to have a try at the phones.

Step 5: If not everyone was able to use a phone, encourage them to do so independently. You might ask them to document whom they contacted and what happened.

Note: This can be a very useful exercise. It presents one of the very few situations in the job search where you can directly observe and modify what a job seeker does or does not do as he or she makes a direct contact with an employer.

DISCUSSION/QUIZ QUESTIONS

Telephone Contacts

1. Is it easy or hard for you to make a real phone contact? Explain.

2. Even if you were never to use the phone contact as a method for getting job leads, what advantages are there to role-playing it aloud with another person?

3. What is the objective of a phone contact? How is it effective in doing that?

4. Is it possible that some employers would not like the approach used in the phone contact? What percentage might like to hear from a potential employee in this way?

5. What were your experiences when using your phone contact with real employers (or in role-playing)? How did you feel about doing it? How did employers or fellow students react to you?

6. How many times should you ask for an interview if your first attempt does not get you one?

7. If you could make the same phone calls discussed above again, how could you improve them?

8. List some alternative objectives for a phone contact if you are not able to reach your primary objective.

9. Describe some times when it might be better to call back rather than press an employer for your primary objective.

10. What should you always do after each phone contact?

CHAPTER SIX

The Interview
For Rave Reviews

The interview is perhaps the most critical event of the job-search process. Much of *The Work Book* is designed to prepare job seekers for doing better in job interviews than they would have done otherwise.

Early in Chapter 6 we bring up what many job seekers fear—problem questions. Our objective is to help students overcome the fear of the most difficult questions they may be asked. This is done by providing them with sample responses.

We also use other techniques. In tennis, research has indicated that athletes can improve their performance by imagining such scenes as the smashing of a tennis ball into the far corner of the opponent's court. The more specific and detailed the mental picture, the better. To improve job seekers' performance, we encourage them to imagine an interview situation in detail. The result is that, in some cases, our job seekers may be more thoroughly prepared than many interviewers (which is a definite advantage).

Chapter 6 of *The Work Book* also builds upon what was learned and drilled in earlier chapters. This repetitious aspect is very important since our intent is to elicit semiautomatic responses that will carry most job seekers through many anxiety-producing interviews. All of our drills are designed to elicit matter-of-fact responses. This is true even where questions designed to gather negative information are involved. Most suggested responses are related in some way to an employer's expectations and frequently use information from JIST cards.

Many "how-to" books dealing with job interviews concentrate on the sensory aspects of the interview—proper dress, eye contact, and related topics. What these materials fail to deal with are the fears of the job seeker, which hamper natural presentation skills. In *The Work Book* we do acknowledge the mechanical aspects of the interview but concentrate on the dynamic interchange that will soon occur between job seekers and employers. (I am certain job seekers using our approach are as well dressed as those using the more traditional approach—and do much better in the interview itself.)

CORE EXERCISE

The Interview

Objective/Rationale
While the telephone contact is primarily a verbal one, job interviews require control of many things other than the voice. Employers will not only hear our job seekers but also see, touch (shake hands with), and smell them (their perfume or after-shave). Physical appearance and grooming become factors, as does the often mystical factor of "body language."

Role-playing is one way to take the students one step closer to the fearful job interview itself. I have repeatedly seen the most prepared job seekers, the ones who read all the assignments and know what to say, do very poorly in their first mock interview. Their second is bad. The third is pretty good, and the quality improves rapidly from there. Tell the group you expect poor performance at first. Nearly everyone is very shy at times. Remember that role-playing can be very hard for some.

Be cautious about raising anyone's anxiety during role-playing. Although I often don't warn the group what will happen next, I've never had anyone refuse to go along. Do follow these tips, though.

- Always find something good about what each job seeker does as an interviewee.
- Let the shy ones be interviewers first.
- Interview a few shy ones yourself. Make sure they succeed.

Procedure

Step 1: Set up the scene. Let no one know what you are really going to do in step 2. Assign someone to be the employer but provide very few instructions other than "Whatever you say or do is okay—you're the employer!" Define the type of job you will be looking for (a waiter/waitress?) and how you found out about the opening. Tell the class you will now leave the room and return as a job seeker.

Step 2: Go outside, close the door or otherwise get out of sight, and "make a shambles" of your appearance—the more outrageous the better. Open the door and go in—or better yet, knock on the door and wait, then knock again.

Step 3: Totally mishandle yourself. Do everything wrong. Act silly. Make inappropriate and exaggerated responses to any serious questions. Demonstrate everything you shouldn't do. After a reasonable period of time doing this, close the interview poorly, too. Say something like, "Gee, I really need a job. Here's 20 cents for you to call me," or something similar.

Step 4: Now that it's over, you can get yourself back together again, smile, and ask everyone how you did. If they think you did just fine, have them read the entire *Work Book* again.

Step 5: This can be a delightful learning experience if done well, since no one could now do worse than you did. Now that everyone is confident that even he or she could do better, proceed to the next step.

Step 6: Ask the students to form groups of three. Each person is to take a turn as a job seeker, an employer, and a critic. The job seeker is to tell the other two what sort of job he or she is looking for, while the employer interviews. Encourage the job seeker to be serious and to do his or her best. Tell the employer to ask tough questions and to avoid making things too easy.

The critic watches. After each interview, the critic and the employer both make comments on the interviewer's performance. There should be few overly picky critics or employers, since their turn is yet to come. Your role is to observe and provide guidance to groups as needed.

Step 7: Have everyone take a turn at each of the three roles. So that all groups will finish at about the same time, keep the slow groups moving and slow down the faster groups.

Step 8: Congratulate everyone on a fine performance. Discuss what they learned and answer any questions that may arise.

Step 9: Optional: More role-playing could be done now or at a later time.

INTERVIEW EXERCISE

Information Interviews

Objective/Rationale

An information interview is not a job interview. In an information interview, a person who is trying to decide just where his or her skills, abilities, and interests would be best used seeks out and talks to people who might be able to help. Perhaps the most thorough review of how to conduct an information interview is found in *What Color Is Your Parachute?* by Richard N. Bolles.

Many people have problems conducting information interviews. The primary problem for job seekers (who really want to find jobs) is to convince themselves that all they really want is information. Some job seekers also use false pretenses when making contact with employers ("I'm not really looking for a job, but . . .").

For these reasons, I've tried to make the approach direct and nondeceptive. The approach encourages job seekers to avoid going to personnel offices when looking for jobs. When doing information interviews, the job seekers go right to the people who would supervise them. Since it is not really an interview for a specific job opening, it permits job seekers to talk to real employers in a low-threat situation. It may also result in very real job offers—not at all by total accident.

Procedure

Step 1: Students are to think of a place where people who have skills and interests similar to theirs might work. It is preferable that it be a small business that is easily accessible. For example, if the job seeker is interested in the electronics business, a TV repair shop would be a good place to contact.

Step 2: Ask if anyone is having difficulty thinking of an appropriate place to contact. If so, ask the group to make suggestions. To ensure that everyone has a place in mind, randomly ask others what their objectives are.

Step 3: Explain that they are looking for information and not a specific job opening. Then describe what they should say and do in the course of an information interview:
- Introduce themselves and tell why they are there.
- Tell the person whom they are interviewing something about themselves. The information should concentrate on their skills, experience, and career interests.
- Ask the person being interviewed
    a. how he or she got started in this job,
    b. what he or she likes best about the work,
    c. what he or she likes least about the work, and
    d. what suggestions he or she has for those who want to work in the field.
- Thank the person and leave.

Step 4: Encourage students to "buddy up" if they wish, particularly if they are interested in the same things or can share transportation.

Step 5: Students should call ahead, ask to speak to the person they wish to see, and explain the reason they want to speak to him or her. If the person is busy, the job seekers should ask for a time when they can call back. The job seekers should be prepared to contact more than one place if necessary.

Step 6: Have the students go out and do an information interview.

Step 7: During the next class, review what happened. Lead a discussion on how the information interview could be used in a job search.

Step 8: Have the job seekers send thank-you notes to those who were interviewed. A JIST card should be included with each letter. (One never knows.)

INTERVIEW EXERCISE

Problem Questions

Objective/Rationale

In this exercise students are again asked to make contact with employers.

Goals

- To lessen participants' anxieties about the interview process
- To reinforce the reliability/credibility of *The Work Book*
- To improve the job seekers' interviewing skills through feedback on the interviewing/hiring experiences of employers
- To turn out job seekers who are aware of problem areas that need to be addressed during an interview
- To decrease job seekers' fears of interviews by showing participants that their job-search knowledge will adequately prepare them for issues raised in interviews

Materials

- Paper, pencils, and erasers
- Phone books
- 3" x 5" cards

Procedure

Step 1: Participants should have read and completed Chapter 6 of *The Work Book* before doing this exercise.

Step 2: Each participant is asked to select three businesses to contact and to make up a 3" x 5" card for each business. On the cards, the job seekers should write the name, location, and phone number of each business. The type of business should also be indicated.

Step 3: Participants are directed to walk into the business and ask to speak to an owner, department head, manager, or personnel director. This person's name and title or area of responsibility should be added to the card.

Step 4: Job seekers should ask their contacts a single question: "What five interview questions pose the most trouble for people whom you've interviewed?" The questions provided should be listed on the cards as well.

Step 5: Use the cards during follow-up instruction. Have the students compare their lists of questions.

Step 6: Ask the students how the interviewer's responses matched content presented in *The Work Book*. Then ask some or all of the following questions. (Perhaps you can add to the list.)
- How did the interviewer act when asked this question?
- Was this the reaction you expected? Explain.
- Compare and contrast the reactions of the people contacted.
- Was the exercise worth the effort expended?

Step 7: Review the Problem Questions section of Chapter 6 in *The Work Book*.

INTERVIEW EXERCISE

Video Interviewing

Objective/Rationale

If you have access to a video camera and playback system, it is a very useful tool to help job seekers improve their interviewing skills. Use it for every group if possible.

Procedure

Step 1: Get all the equipment set up and operating correctly before the session begins. If a group member is familiar with video equipment, put that person in charge of setup and camera operation to allow you to do other things.

Step 2: Do the core exercise as described above. The differences related to the camera are fairly obvious and need no comment.

Step 3: You can replay the tape of your interview for laughs, but this is optional.

Step 4: Ask for volunteers for the roles of employer and job seeker. If no one volunteers, assign a more able person as the first job seeker—anyone can be the employer. Explain that the employer is not being evaluated and can do whatever he or she wants. Because it is a learning experience, the employer should not make things too difficult or at all silly. He or she should ask difficult questions of the job seeker but not make the interview unrealistically hard. Encourage the employer to react as he or she really might to the way the job seeker handles things. The job seeker should simply try to do his or her best. Others in the group are to watch and take notes on whether the job seeker could have done better in presenting him- or herself.

Step 5: Have the first pair role-play the interview. The job seeker should leave the room and knock on the door as part of the exercise. Help set the scene before the exercise begins by having the job seeker decide the sort of position being applied for, how he or she found out about it, and what sort of an organization it is in. The interviewer is to accept these decisions as facts and conduct the interview accordingly. The actors should be told to end the interview after about ten minutes. Tell the camera to roll and instruct the two students to begin the interview.

Step 6: Let the interview happen with as little interference as possible from you. You may need to help end it after about ten minutes or help keep it going a bit longer if your pair is shy.

Note: Rather than having the first interview in front of the whole group, you could divide a larger group into two or more smaller ones. Everyone should get to interview as a job seeker before the camera, if at all possible, but larger groups get more practice time in smaller subgroups. Select a more experienced or competent leader for the subgroups to allow you to circulate.

Step 7: After the interview is finished, ask the group for specific things the job seeker did well or might have done better. The employer could also be asked how he or she felt about the job seeker's performance. Realize that you have made the job seeker very vulnerable to ridicule, and do not allow anyone to be too critical. Defend the job seeker by pointing out what he or she did well and reminding the others that this was the first interview. Their turn will come! After some initial discussion, play back segments of the tape and continue to encourage discussion by stopping the tape as appropriate.

Step 8: Wrap up the first role-play on a positive note, thank the two brave souls who went first, and move on to the next pair.

DISCUSSION/QUIZ QUESTIONS

The Interview

1. Name at least two ways you could create a negative impression either before you go into an interview or in the first few seconds of one. Explain why this could affect whether or not you are offered a job.

2. If you are asked, "How much money do you expect to make?" in an interview, give two ways you might respond. Explain why you would handle the question that way.

3. Laws restrict many employers from making a hiring decision based on certain things they might know about a job seeker. Name three of these things and explain why these laws might have been made.

4. Many employers want to know about your personal situation, such as whether you are married, have children, and other matters. What good reason would an employer have for wanting to know this information? Give a response you might make if asked these questions that would give the employers the information they seek in a way that helps you get an offer.

5. What are the steps in the proof-by-example method? Give an interview response that you might use that includes all the steps.

6. Answer the question "What is your major weakness?" in a way that answers the question honestly but also helps you create a positive impression.

7. Why do interviewers often ask, "Won't you tell me about yourself?" What kind of answer takes advantage of this question?

8. List at least four questions you could ask in an interview that would help indicate you are a good worker.

9. What are the most important types of skills to describe in an interview? Why?

10. What is the name of the follow-up technique recommended at the end of the interview? Describe it in detail.

CHAPTER SEVEN

Finding Job Leads
Uncovering the Hidden Jobs

Most people assume they know more about finding jobs than they really do. Demonstrating this, however, is difficult because people often can't see the effects of their erroneous beliefs. Apparently, learning more about job seeking is much like learning to care for children properly before one has them—not too many people bother, but few would argue that it makes sense to do so.

The fact is that people are incredibly ignorant about how to find jobs or which techniques are the most effective. I, for example, went through graduate school, changed careers several times, and became a father before I read my first book on how to find a job. I'm sure this situation has improved somewhat, but I'm also certain that most people still don't have the faintest idea of the facts *The Work Book* outlines. Consider this knowledge a gift from you to your students which, if acted upon, can affect their lives.

The belief that the best way to find jobs is to send out resumes or to go to personnel offices and fill out applications is one that can cause major problems for your students. You should instill in them the idea that these are only a few of the available techniques—and not the most effective ones at that.

Out of habit, you yourself might unconsciously discuss the job search in terms of the traditional, more passive methods. I even get caught up in the trap when I have told someone about a variety of effective techniques and he or she then asks, "Well, how do you get past the personnel office?" The correct response might be "Why are you even talking about places with personnel offices?" Most small businesses, which happen to hire the majority of job seekers in the United States, don't even have them. Even if job seekers go to a place that has a personnel office, who says they have to stop there? If there's a "fence," they need advice on bypassing it; if there isn't one, they should simply walk past. Of course, it is much easier when job seekers have set up an appointment beforehand. This approach is particularly functional when dealing with larger organizations.

You may have wondered why the topic of job-search techniques was ignored until Chapter 7 of *The Work Book*. The answer is that it wasn't. Information about finding job leads was sprinkled throughout earlier chapters, and it is all pulled together in Chapter 7.

Notice that I use job leads rather than job openings. Our objective is to emphasize the *source* of knowledge about where jobs might be—that is, people. If we can get our job seekers to meet people and present themselves well, the invisible jobs become accessible. In summary, job seekers should

- identify people to whom they can talk,
- present themselves well,
- ask their contacts if they know anyone else who might be interested in helping them, and
- follow up.

The content of this chapter primarily involves the transfer of information. As such, some lecture is unavoidable when presenting the material to a class. However, the content is of great interest and can form the basis for discussion and other activities.

CORE EXERCISE

Job Leads (Traditional Sources)

Objective/Rationale

Most people, although aware of a variety of ways for discovering job leads, rarely have an accurate sense of how effective each method is. The following exercise is a good one to give as both pre- and posttest.

Procedure

Step 1: Devise a very simple pretest. It should ask questions that are based on Chapter 7 of *The Work Book*. The information from Bulletin 1886 that is found at the beginning of the chapter is a good source of information for questions. A question that might be asked is "Of all the people in the United States who work, what percentage of them use want ads (employment agencies, sending out resumes, asking friends or relatives) to find jobs?"

Step 2: Ask the group to hold on to their written responses for now.

Step 3: On a blackboard or flip chart, write down all reasonable responses that the class gives to this question: "Tell me as many ways to find jobs as you can think of."

Step 4: If your group is average, the responses will include most of these:

- Want ads
- Friends
- Relatives
- Personnel offices
- School placement offices
- State employment offices
- Sending out resumes
- Private employment agencies

If the job seekers don't think of some of the above sources, add them yourself. Also, add any other sources you or they might wish to have on the list.

Step 5: Refer to the diagram on the facing page, entitled "How People Get Jobs." It translates the more complex data from Bulletin 1886 into easily understood pie charts. For now, this diagram is for your information only.

Step 6: Each technique cited in step 4 and its effectiveness rate should be written on the board. For example:

Want ads   10–14%
Agencies   9–12%
Other   7–11%

Step 7: On a separate flip chart or a clean section of the board, make a large circle. Then, make the circle into a pie chart. Refer to the "How People Get Jobs" diagram. Strongly emphasize that traditional job-seeking methods account for only about one-third of all jobs found!

Step 8: Review the importance of informal methods of finding job leads. Stress that such methods are very effective and should be used extensively in most job searches.

JOB LEADS EXERCISE

Friends and Relatives

Objective/Rationale

Bulletin 1886 indicates that friends and relatives are the second most effective source of job leads (after direct employer contact). In fact, nearly 30 percent of new employees find their jobs in this way. So, it is essential that your students learn to contact friends and relatives systematically.

Procedure

Step 1: For a form to use, refer to the Networking Form in Chapter 9 of *The Work Book*. Extra forms will be required in most cases.

Step 2: Have each student list all his or her relatives of working age who live in the vicinity. These people should be listed even if they do not presently work.

Step 3: After step 2 has been completed, define *friend* as any person of working age who meets these basic criteria:

- Recognizes the job seeker (or could do so, if necessary), even if not by name.
- Would probably be willing to talk to the job seeker, if the need arose.
- Does not dislike the job seeker.

How People Get Jobs

Granovetter[1]
(Professional-Technical-Managerial)

Mark S. Granovetter, a sociologist at Harvard University, investigated how people got jobs. His study included professional, technical, and managerial workers who had recently found jobs. The chart shows the methods by which their jobs had been obtained.

Granovetter's data also indicated that of the people who found jobs through personal contacts, 43% had new positions created for them. Granovetter concluded, "Personal contacts are of paramount importance in connecting people with jobs. Better jobs are found through contacts, and the best jobs, the ones with the highest pay and prestige and affording the greatest satisfaction to those in them, are most apt to be filled in this way."

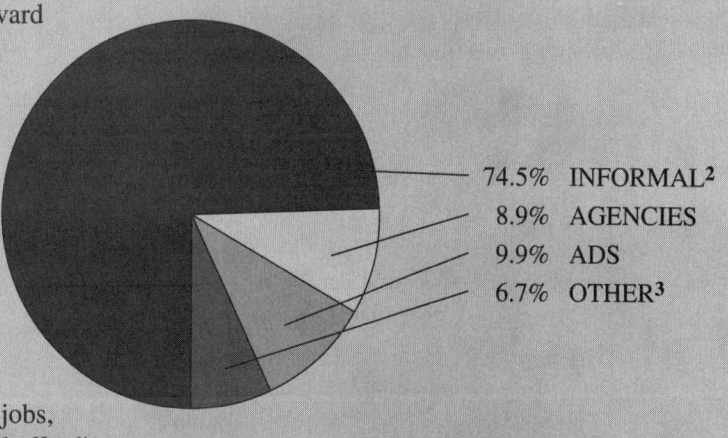

74.5% INFORMAL[2]
8.9% AGENCIES
9.9% ADS
6.7% OTHER[3]

U.S. Department of Labor[4]
(Blue-Collar and White-Collar)

The U.S. Government conducted a comprehensive survey in 1973 to determine how American workers find jobs. The study included all categories of wage and salary workers, except farm workers—from professionals and administrators, to construction workers and mechanics. The sample consisted of 10.4 million men and women who found new jobs, and the chart shows the methods by which their jobs had been obtained.

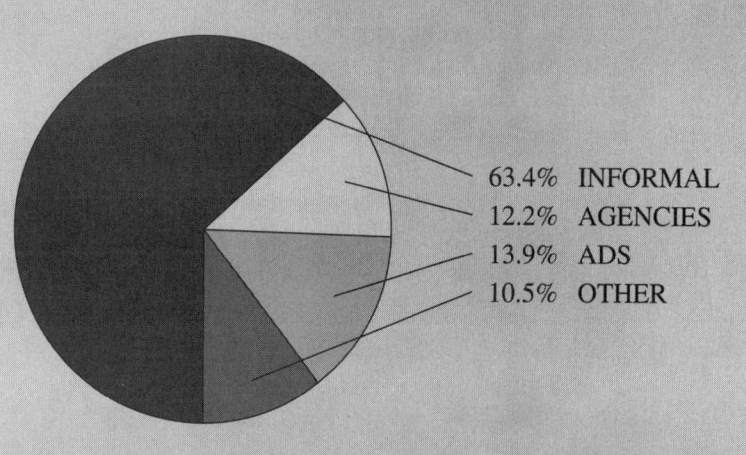

63.4% INFORMAL
12.2% AGENCIES
13.9% ADS
10.5% OTHER

---

1   Granovetter, *Getting a Job: A Study of Contacts and Careers*, Harvard University Press, Cambridge, 1974.
2   *Informal* methods of job finding are those whereby the job seekers exercise their own initiative in building on personal contacts and making themselves known to potential employers. They are differentiated from "formal" methods, which rely on advertisements and/or employment agencies.
3   *Other* is a residual category that encompasses such methods of job finding as trade-union hiring and civil service.
4   *Jobseeking Methods Used by American Workers*, U.S. Department of Labor, Bureau of Labor Statistics, Bulletin 1886, 1975.

Point out that this definition fits most people we know. So, nearly everyone fits the description—the people at the local gas station, grocery store, arcade, etc.—as well as persons who are more traditionally defined as friends.

Step 4: Ask everyone to think of 10–15 friends (as defined). Each job seeker should then write down the names of these people, if known. If names are not known, the job seeker should identify them in some other way ("the guy who fixes my ten-speed" or "the woman who cashiers at the gas station").

Step 5: Have everyone now choose at least two people from his or her list to contact.

Step 6: Instruct each student to visit the two persons chosen prior to the next session. With each person, they should follow these guidelines:

- They should set up an appointment so they can have at least 45 minutes of the person's uninterrupted time. The job seekers should say they are looking for a job and want some advice.
- Once there, they should briefly explain the nature of the job they are looking for and relate their skills and experiences to the job objective that has been chosen. (This would be a good time to give out a JIST card.)
- The job seekers should ask for suggestions, advice, and ideas on how one might go about finding openings in the friend's field. (For more background on information interviews, see Chapter 7 of *The Work Book*.)
- Because the job seekers want to learn something, they should listen carefully.
- If it doesn't come up naturally, students are to ask the names of anyone the friend knows who
  a. hires people with the job seeker's interests and skills,
  b. knows something about the job seeker's areas of interest and may be willing to speak with him/her, or
  c. might know someone else who could be of help.

For follow-up purposes, students should be sure to write down the contact's name and any other available information. (A version of the Direct Contact List found in Chapter 9 of *The Work Book* could be adapted for use here.)

Step 7: The job seekers should thank the friend and leave.

Step 8: Depending on your inclinations, their energy levels, and the time available, the job seekers could also follow up on the referrals gained in step 6.

Step 9: As homework, have students research the phone numbers of other friends and relatives on their lists. Again, they could follow up on these contacts.

Step 10: In the next class or session, discuss what happened. Which techniques worked best? Did anyone find a job opening? What was the percentage of success in finding a good lead or an opening itself? Was the opening advertised?

Step 11: Have everyone write and send a thank-you note to the friends and relatives contacted. Again, a JIST card should be included.

Step 12: To wrap up the exercise, emphasize that using friends and relatives as a contact base for job leads is very important. Since people are so likely to forget this point, however, you must do everything you can to structure their thinking toward using this source. Remind the group that because they can return to see the same person and because they should get the name(s) of one or more referrals each time, they can develop extensive lists of job leads.

JOB LEADS EXERCISE

Networking

Objective/Rationale

In many ways, this exercise is similar to the one in which friends and relatives were used as job-lead sources. Here, we present the concept of developing a network of people who will help job seekers discover unadvertised job openings.

Procedure

Step 1: Review the concept of the "hidden" job market. Emphasize that the people who do know of these unadvertised job openings are just people, not some "superbeings."

Step 2: Explain that our objective is to crack the hidden job market. On a blackboard or flip chart, draw one small circle near the top. Say that this represents one person who meets these criteria:
- He or she will talk to the job seeker.
- He or she knows people.

Yes, this does include nearly everyone.

Step 3: Your students' objectives are to
- meet these people,
- present themselves well,
- tell these people something about their interests,
- learn something, and
- get the names of at least two others who may also be willing to speak with them.

Step 4: On the board next to the circle, feel free to write in content from steps 2 or 3. Now, draw two more small circles under the first, and connect them with lines as shown below. Explain that if the job seekers meet their objective, they will get the names of two more people. These people could then be contacted ("Hello, John Smith suggested I give you a call.").

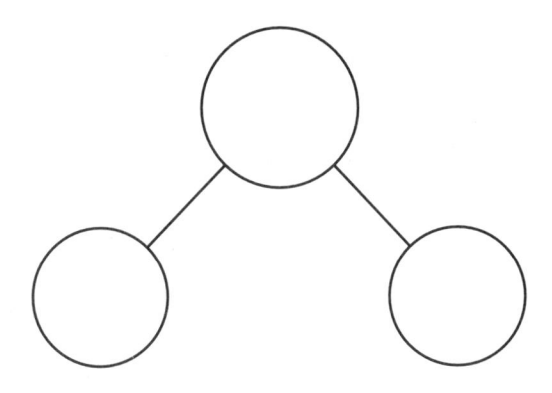

Step 5: Under each new circle, draw two more and connect them with new lines. (See the example at the top of the next column.) Keep adding more and more circles and lines while explaining how many more people previously unknown are entering into a network of contacts. Literally hundreds can be added quickly.

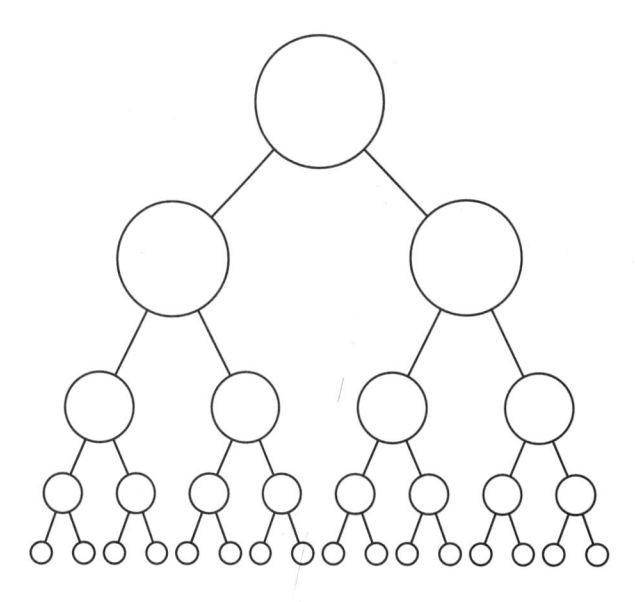

Step 6: Point out that one of these new contacts will know of a job opening. Because of the potentially large number of contacts, it is essential that all referrals be documented and followed up in a routine and systematic way. Tools for doing this are included in Chapter 9 of *The Work Book*.

Step 7: Have everyone select a target person and meet with him or her prior to the next session. Any area of interest can be pursued; it does not have to be job related.

Step 8: At the next session, discuss the results. Suggest that 40 or more contacts may have to be made before a job offer is received; but, at the rate of only two contacts per day, most job seekers will get a job offer within a month. (Based on our experience, this is true in most situations. It's that simple.)

JOB LEADS EXERCISE

The Yellow Pages

Objective/Rationale

The Work Book provides information on using the Yellow Pages as a source of job leads. This is an extremely good source for finding a wide variety of outlets for almost any skill. Knowing about the Yellow Pages, however, and actually using them are two separate things. This exercise is designed to accustom students to using this valuable resource.

Procedure

Step 1: Round up enough Yellow Page directories so that each group of three or fewer students can have one. (Or you could simply ask everyone to bring in directories.)

Step 2: Thoroughly review with the class the content of *The Work Book* that relates to the use of the Yellow Pages (Chapter 7). Make sure that everyone understands how the Yellow Pages can be used as a source of job leads. Also, review the not-so-obvious physical layout (index, cross-references, etc.) of the Yellow Pages themselves.

Step 3: Have each person refer to the index of the Yellow Pages and find five headings that evoke a positive response to the question "Would this type of an organization possibly have some use for a person with my skills and interests?" The obvious headings are not always the best, so encourage some creative thinking. Students may wish to begin in the index under A and ask the question in respect to each heading.

Step 4: When each person has at least five index headings, ask students to list them in their order of importance. The students should use the Yellow Pages Prospect List in Chapter 7 as a model.

Step 5: Have everyone now turn to the Yellow Pages section for one or more of the headings selected. The data on specific companies listed there should then be transferred onto a Direct Contact List like the one shown in Chapter 9 of *The Work Book*. Have the students make extra forms as necessary.

Step 6: Each student now has found a way to develop new sources of job leads. Each of these leads can now be pursued. Techniques described in Chapters 5 and 6 of *The Work Book* may be used here as well. Remind students that their objectives are the same as those outlined earlier—

- to get an interview (even if no job is open),
- to present themselves well,
- to learn something, and
- to get the names of two others who may also speak with them.

DISCUSSION/QUIZ QUESTIONS

Finding Job Leads

1. List the job-seeking techniques called "visible" and the percentages of people who find their jobs using them.
2. Name the major job-seeking techniques for finding "hidden" jobs and the percentages of people who find employment using them.
3. What are the two most used job-search techniques? Are any other techniques more effective? Explain.
4. What is the "hidden" job market?
5. Is an information interview the right type of interview to use if you know what type of job you want? Explain.
6. From a job seeker's point of view, why is a personnel office not always the best place to look for a job?
7. How effective is the _____ (insert whatever name your state gives to the state-run unemployment office)? How and when should a job seeker use it?
8. List five sources to use in making a list of employers to contact for hidden job openings.
9. Name two traditional job-search techniques, and describe how a well-trained job seeker might use them.
10. Describe networking in detail. Give examples of how it works.

CHAPTER EIGHT

Resumes
Make Your REZ-oo-MAY Pay

I have mixed feelings about resumes and, therefore, considered not including a chapter on them. What appears in *The Work Book* is a definite compromise in some respects. For example, there has been little attempt to present a comprehensive view of resume formats. Here is the rationale:

- For most users of *The Work Book,* a resume is a very poor job-finding tool. Their time might be better spent elsewhere.

- Because the resume is seen by many to be an indispensable job-search tool, preparing and using one can easily consume much of a job seeker's time and effort (in spite of any warnings given).

- The topic of resumes is a very complex one. Once a discussion on them has begun, it is very difficult to end.

- Numerous books have been written about resumes. (Two good ones are Tom Jackson's *The Perfect Resume* and Richard Lathrop's *Who's Hiring Who.*) Unfortunately, many are very poorly done and offer ineffective job-search advice. The good ones provide far more detail than *The Work Book* does. Those can be used as references for a person who wants more information on the topic.

Even though there were many reasons to exclude a section on resumes, one was included anyway. Here's why:

- Many employers ask for resumes, particularly for some occupations.
- Many job seekers want to have a resume.
- Resumes can be helpful, if used correctly.
- Resumes do provide a good framework for organizing certain data.
- It is better for job seekers to make up resumes early on, rather than avoid the job search for lack of one.

The chapter is divided into several major sections. The first section presents the idea that resumes are only one job-search tool out of many. Resumes are then related to an employer's expectations. The second section helps the job seeker build a very simple (but acceptable) resume. The objective of this approach is to help the job seeker develop a resume quickly. If a better one is desired, it can be written later. In the interim, a resume would be available. The chapter uses a building-block approach: increasingly sophisticated resumes are presented along with tips for their construction.

Putting together a more sophisticated resume may be beyond the abilities of many people. In those cases the assistance of a professional may be needed. Whether it is written by the job seeker or by a professional, a sophisticated resume must be based on a thorough understanding of the job seeker's skills and job objective. It must also show a much-better-than-average grasp of the language. My general suggestions regarding resumes are as follows:

- If a job seeker wants one or may need one, encourage him or her to make up a simple, chronological resume first. It should be error-free and attractive. A job objective and a few "improvements" are desirable only if they can be done in a one-night resume-writing project.

- The job seeker should have about 50 copies of the simple resume printed on quality paper.

- Only then should a more sophisticated resume be written in the evenings. In the meantime, the simple resume can be used.

CORE EXERCISE

Making a Resume

Objective/Rationale

You and the class can talk or read about resumes, but there is no substitute for putting one together.

Procedure

Step 1: Have everyone read Chapter 8 of *The Work Book*. For homework, each person should write content to be included in a simple resume. You can decide whether or not other resume basics, such as a job objective, should be included. Unless everyone has access to a typewriter or a computer, a neat, hand-printed version should suffice for now.

Step 2: In the following class, have the students exchange resumes. Each resume should be critiqued from the point of view of an employer looking for an excuse to screen out applicants. Is the resume sloppy in appearance? Are there spelling errors? Is there poor grammar? Did the writer make negative statements? Errors should be circled and notes made on the resume.

Step 3: Have the resumes returned to their respective writers. Before initiating a discussion, remind everyone that making a good resume has little to do with the quality of on-the-job performance. For example, a poor speller can make an excellent executive. However, remind the class that employers will always act based on their perceptions. Flawed resumes will not impress them.

Step 4: Discuss any problems, observations, or questions related to the preparation and use of resumes.

Step 5: Have all students revise their resumes, taking into consideration the feedback received. A final version should be submitted (this might be done at the next session).

Step 6: Find a way to have all resumes typed or printed out. As an option, you could require that the completed and corrected versions be submitted for your review. Photocopies or printed copies of the resumes should be made if your students plan on using them in the near future.

RESUME EXERCISE
Collecting Resumes

Objective/Rationale

The examination of other people's resumes can provide job seekers with a learning experience.

Procedure

Step 1: As homework, ask each student to gather a designated number of different resumes. The resumes can be obtained from any source, but they must be either real resumes or photocopies of real ones. Examples from books are not allowed.

Step 2: At the next session, have students discuss the ways in which they found the resumes that were brought in. Encourage the group to speak about any significant experiences that happened during this process.

Step 3: Each student is then to review each resume he or she has collected and write a brief critique of it—one page maximum. This exercise could be done as homework.

Step 4: The best and the worst features of the various resumes collected should be presented by each student. Specific points should be cited ("This resume was messy and didn't have a telephone number or address on it.").

Step 5: Discuss what was learned and answer any questions that are raised.

RESUME EXERCISE
A Survey of Employers

Objective/Rationale

In this exercise, students are to contact employers directly and ask them several questions about resumes. Besides providing experience in dealing with employers, the activity will give job seekers information that can be compared with views presented in *The Work Book*.

Procedure

Step 1: Have the class come up with a list of about five questions that can be used in an employer survey dealing with attitudes towards resumes. This activity could be done in groups of three or four. Here are some possible questions:

- What are the three most frequent faults you find in the resumes you see?
- When making a decision to hire or not hire, which is the more important to you—the interview or the resume?
- Can a person who has no resume get in to see you? Suppose someone does and you're impressed with him or her. Would you then ask for a resume?

- How can a young person (a career changer, a reentering homemaker, etc.) who doesn't have a lot of formal, related work experience construct a resume that will overcome this problem?
- Does a resume usually help you to screen an applicant in or out?

Step 2: Clarify and simplify the questions so that they are quantifiable and easy for the employer to answer. Ask each student to write down the questions, or, if you so desire, have a form developed.

Step 3: Have each student (or pair of students) survey one (or more) employer(s). The student(s) should record the name of each employer as well as the answers given.

Step 4: The responses should be gathered and quantified. A summary of the results could easily be developed in a class session.

Step 5: Review and discuss the findings, results, experiences, observations, and conclusions of the survey. Students might compare and contrast the conclusions with the suggestions presented in Chapter 8 of *The Work Book*.

DISCUSSION/QUIZ QUESTIONS

Resumes

1. Is a resume a good tool to use in getting interviews? Explain.
2. What are the major types of resumes? Give examples of job seekers who might use each type.
3. Is it necessary to put personal information on a resume? Explain.
4. Why might some employers not like a nontraditional skills, or functional, resume?
5. Describe at least three situations where a resume would not be needed in order to get an interview or job offer.
6. On your resume, which is better—to simply list all your duties from previous jobs or to emphasize your accomplishments?
7. Describe two ways that you could handle references on your resume and the advantages and disadvantages of each.
8. A resume can make an impression about you before it is even read. List common resume errors made by job seekers that create a negative impression.
9. Other than sending your resume to a personnel department, name as many other uses for a resume in your job search as you can.
10. Is it wise to delay looking for a job until your resume is as good as it can be? Explain.

Chapter 8   Resumes

CHAPTER NINE

Organizing Your Job Search
Ready, Set, Go!

Knowing how to do something and actually doing it well are two very different processes. Having been a job seeker myself and having worked with numerous job seekers, I know that the distinction between learning and doing has become very clear to me. Many of the exercises presented in this guide are action-oriented. They require students to use what they have learned. Unfortunately, the support system of a structured class and the imposed discipline applied by a good teacher are gone once students are on their own. As a result, one of three basic things is likely to happen:

1. Some students, by applying what they have learned, will find a desirable job quickly.
2. Other students will use traditional job-search techniques. Their interviewing skills will be better than average, but they will act as if they know nothing of using such nontraditional, effective techniques such as contacting friends, relatives, and small businesses and using the Yellow Pages.
3. After a few unsuccessful contacts, many will almost give up. They will spend few hours per week on their job search and, consequently, get few interviews.

You've succeeded with the first group of students. You've given them something that is quite valuable—information on how to look for a job—and they have followed your advice. For those students in the second group (which includes, I fear, many who are taught by some of the best instructors), you might wish to make one last attempt to help them organize their efforts into a job-search plan. Chapter 9 of *The Work Book* will assist you in this effort. Students in the third group also have an obvious need to structure their time more productively. With them, do what you can. Looking for a job is not an easy task for anyone; it is often very discouraging. Negative feedback, which is built into the process itself, frequently causes job seekers to reduce their efforts.

The objective of Chapter 9 of *The Work Book* is to provide a routine that will commit a job seeker to doing specific activities that will, if followed, help all three groups of job seekers. The self-motivated will have a plan that organizes their efforts more productively. Those who have a tendency to use traditional techniques will be encouraged to put them into their proper context and to use other methods as well. A job-search plan that sets specific objectives and schedules will provide positive reinforcement that will enable some job seekers to overcome the activity-stopping discouragement experienced by so many.

The importance of your assistance to students as they outline and start to implement their individual job-search programs can't be overemphasized. This will be your last opportunity to monitor the progress of your people. Take the role seriously.

CORE EXERCISE

The Job Search (Getting It Done)

Objective/Rationale

This exercise will lead students through the activities in Chapter 9. For the most part, the chapter is self-explanatory. It should be reviewed in detail; questions and discussion are to be encouraged.

If possible, each student should complete all forms in Chapter 9. If you don't want to use the forms as they are, they can be easily adapted to fit the students' needs. Because many variables may exist (such as the amount of available time), the minimum objective is that each job seeker should become familiar with the concept of a job-search plan.

Procedure

Step 1: Assign Chapter 9 as homework.

Step 2: For the next session, have everyone bring to class a copy of the Yellow Pages. Also ask the students to think of questions they may want to ask about the chapter.

Step 3: Ask the students how Chapter 9 might help them find a job in less time. This can be asked of groups of 3–5 students. The topic can then be discussed within these small groups. Each group might be asked to make a list of the various points brought out in the discussion. The lists could then be read to the entire group.

Step 4: Slowly "walk through" each part of the chapter. Encourage students and clarify problems.

Step 5: Review the sample Daily Job-Search Plan in detail.

Step 6: Present the Daily/Weekly Job-Search Calendar as a framework that each student will use when writing his or her own job-search plan. Then, ask the job seekers to start on their plans. Unless the creation of a plan is assigned as homework, some quiet time in class should be allowed for this purpose. Encourage the use of pencils, so erasures can be made as the plan is changed. You could require students to present their plans in small groups; subsequent revisions can then be made based on the feedback received. If a full-time job is sought, you should encourage each student to spend at least 25 hours per week on the job search.

Step 7: The data on the Direct-Contact List can easily be put on 3" x 5" cards. Since many contacts can be made by a reasonably active job seeker, the cards soon become essential memory aids for follow-up. Suggest that 30 new cards be prepared prior to each day's telephone session. A reasonably active job seeker can easily make 30 phone calls per day. (If possible, to get started, 30 cards or so might be developed in class.)

Step 8: The Networking Form and Follow-Up Card are simple forms for collecting and following up on a frequently overlooked (but very important) source of job leads. Students may use 3" x 5" cards to organize data on these forms as well.

Step 9: Wrap up the activity. If this is the end of the class, students will now be completely on their own. Review the fundamentals and be open for questions. Wish the job seekers luck, but point out (as my grandfather often did) that the harder you work the luckier you get.

DISCUSSION/QUIZ QUESTIONS

Organizing Your Job Search

1. How many hours per week does the average job seeker spend looking for a job? How many hours per week are recommended as a minimum?

2. If you follow the suggestions given in *The Work Book*, how many interviews per day will you try to obtain? How does this compare with the average job seeker's activity, and what is the likely result?

3. Describe the basic daily schedule for an active job search as outlined in the book. Give specific times and activities.

4. After an interview, what is the first thing to do after getting home (or as soon as possible)? Why?

5. Describe a simple system to organize your contacts for follow-up by date.

6. How can you use the Yellow Pages of the phone book to get job leads?

7. Describe the basic form used to keep track of job leads developed from networking activities. Give details of how it works.

8. Name five groups of people you can contact as part of your networking activities.

9. When are good times to send a thank-you note and why?

10. While it is a hard technique for some people to use, why are telephone contacts emphasized as part of a daily job-search plan?

ANNOTATED BIBLIOGRAPHY

There is a bewildering variety of job-search material out there now in libraries and bookstores. Unfortunately, most of it is not very good, and it is difficult to separate the wheat from the chaff. What follows are my opinionated comments on what I like.

I've spent many hours poring over various materials through the years, and the things I describe here are some of the best. Most are also reasonably priced, though some are fairly obscure and not likely to be available from your local library. Your friendly research librarian, however, should be able to get them elsewhere.

Assessment Materials

The Work Book does not provide career assessment content. It assumes that the reader has a job objective of some sort. It is likely that you will need to help some people define or refine their objectives as part of what you do. So, here are some resources to help.

Books

A Counselor's Guide to Vocational Guidance Instruments. Jerome Kapes and Marjorie Mastie. Alexandria, VA: American Association for Counseling & Development, 1982. This book provides reviews of various tests. I don't always agree with the reviews, but everyone is entitled to his or her opinion.

The Janus Job Planner. Wing Jew and Robert Tong. Hayward, CA: Janus Book Publishers, 1987. A unique book because of its low reading level. While written at the third-grade level, it can also be used by persons with much higher reading levels, making it especially effective for use with heterogeneous groups.

Life Plan: A Practical Guide to Successful Career Planning. Louise W. Schrank. Chicago: National Textbook Co., 1980. A thorough book that would be good for use in a course. The reading level is modest, and it uses a workbook format to lead the reader to a well-defined job objective.

The Mental Measurements Yearbook. Oscar K. Burors, Ed. Lincoln, NE: University of Nebraska Press, 1978. Many big libraries have this. It is a rather stuffy but objective source of data on various tests, including vocational ones.

Tests

I prefer tests that are self-scoring and involve the test taker in a learning experience. That is why I do not include the "traditional" interest tests in this section (such as the Kuder, for example.) Besides, most tests are restricted, and many instructors are not well enough qualified to ensure their proper use.

As with all tests, you should carefully read their professional manuals before trying to use them. I also suggest that you take the tests yourself. (How else can you understand what you are asking of your job seekers?) The tests recommended here and on page xiii are self-scored and can be interpreted by most adults with just a bit of explanation.

The Jackson Vocational Interest Survey (the JVIS), published by the Research Psychologist's Press, Port Huron, MI, is a more traditional and less user friendly test than the Self-Directed Search or the Career Decision-Making System. It provides a well-researched basis for selecting occupations. It takes about an hour to get through and can be self-scored. Interpretation of the results, however, will take help from an instructor.

Job-Search Books

Most of the better-known books on job seeking were written for people who buy books in bookstores. That is a substantial but relatively restricted group. These books are fun to read, consist primarily of narrative, and are written for people with good reading and comprehension skills. However, they are not usually effective as the basis for a group study or program because they are often not

Annotated Bibliography 45

concrete enough, and many provide advice that is not all that useful for an outcome-oriented job search. Also, many are downright misleading or poorly informed in their advice. Those I have left out of this admittedly short list.

The Complete Job Search Handbook. Howard Figler. New York: Henry Holt & Co., 1988. A thorough source of ideas for job seekers and trainers.

Guerilla Tactics in the Job Market. Tom Jackson. New York: Bantam Books, Inc., 1978. This has been a popular book for years now because of the many useful techniques it provides.

Job Finding Fast. J. Michael Farr. Mission Hills, CA: Glencoe/McGraw-Hill, 1990. This book is longer than *The Work Book* and has content to help identify job objectives, more examples, and a higher reading level. It should be very effective as the basis for a course and should seem familiar if you are comfortable with the content of *The Work Book*.

The Perfect Resume. Tom Jackson. New York: Doubleday & Co., Inc., 1981. While I think resumes are terribly overrated as a job-search tool, this is a well-done resume book. Use it to supplement *The Work Book* chapter on resumes for the relatively few who need more sophisticated advice.

Sweaty Palms: The Neglected Art of Being Interviewed. H. Anthony Medley. Berkeley, CA: Ten Speed Press, 1993. Witty, fun, good advice, and enjoyable to read.

What Color Is Your Parachute? Richard Nelson Bolles. Berkeley: Ten Speed Press, 1994. This is the best-selling job-search book of all time. Since it's revised annually, you really ought to read a new edition if you've not done that for awhile. It is an excellent book for career changers and has a wealth of exercises to help identify the things so often overlooked in making a vocational choice such as values, skills, and much more. The reading level can be handled by most high school graduates with good reading skills.

Who's Hiring Who. Richard Lathrop. Berkeley: Ten Speed Press, 1989. One of my favorites. It has concrete advice on job-search methods and a good resume section. Very readable and helpful.

Career Information Books

The Department of Labor and Glencoe/McGraw-Hill produce a number of very important resources that are among the best in their category—at any price. The first three books listed below are DOL publications; the last is a Glencoe/McGraw-Hill reference book.

The Dictionary of Occupational Titles. The *DOT* lists over 20,000 jobs and important details for each. It is as much fun to read as a phone book but indispensable as a reference tool.

The Guide to Occupational Exploration. The guide cross-references all the *DOT* codes in useful ways for career exploration. The system takes a bit of getting used to, but the information is worth the effort.

The Occupational Outlook Handbook. The *OOH* lists many fewer jobs than the DOT, but it includes the ones that roughly 75 percent of the population have. It is interesting and easy to read. A revision comes out every two years and includes new salary ranges and occupational projections for each job covered. You definitely need to have one of these for your own information and for your job seekers to browse.

The Worker Trait Group Guide. This is the book for you if you need something like the *OOH* but at a lower reading level. There really isn't anything else like it.

Instructor Materials

Here are some suggestions for your own library:

The Job Market: What Ails It and What Needs to Be Done About It to Reduce Unemployment. Richard Lathrop. Washington: National Center for Job Market Studies, 1978. A small book but packed with data supporting a rationale for sensible training in job-research skills as a national policy. I use the data all the time to sound reasonably well-informed when making presentations.

Job Power: The Young People's Job Finding Guide. Bernard Haldane. Washington: Acropolis Books, 1982. Hard to find and subject to going out of print, this book does an effective job of providing ideas and exercises for use in group assessment and skills identification.

Looking for Work in the New Economy. Robert Wegmann et al. Salt Lake City: Olympus Publishing Co., 1986. A thoroughly researched book on where the economy is taking us and some suggested approaches you or your organization should take in training job seekers to be prepared.